Aletheia Pyralis Publishers

For information about special discounts available
for bulk purchases, sales promotions, fund-raising
and educational needs, please email:
devyaschildren@gmail.com.

http://www.juliecgilbert.com/
https://sites.google.com/view/juliecgilbert-
writer/

Love Science Fiction or Mystery?

Choose your adventure!
Visit: **http://www.juliecgilbert.com/**

For details on getting free books.

Dedications:

Thin Black Road: For my friends Jenny Parsons and Marie Graham.

Just Like You: To Timothy Sparvero, awesome illustrator.

My Champion: To my friend Cara, thanks for encouraging me to rewrite and publish these.

To Barbara for inspiring the cover idea.

Table of Contents:

Dedications:
1. Thin Black Road
2. Burden Not Seen
3. To My Former Master
4. Not What I'd Pictured
5. Why the Tears?
6. Speak Soft Words
7. My Days are Numbered
8. No Sleep
9. Times of Trouble
10. Is There Anything …
11. Walk On
12. God Will have the Last Word
13. Beautiful Day
14. Deep-seated Peace
15. Am I Hiding My Heart
16. Rain Down Wisdom
17. Every Moment
18. Worry Won't Win Any Wars
19. Driving Me Crazy
20. Freely
21. Listen
22. Better
23. Dancing Sun
24. Made to Praise
25. Peace of God
26. Right Place to Sing
27. Light in My Eyes
28. We Needed a Hero
29. Chosen One

30. Move, Mountain, Move
31. End and Beginning
32. Best Day
33. Let Him In
34. Dance to Life
35. The Long Story
36. Never Alone
37. Somewhere Today
38. Grim Day
39. Lost Ones
40. New Title
41. Money Can and Cannot
42. God Doesn't Know How to Fail
43. Enemy
44. When You're Weary
45. Mountain of Troubles
46. Had Enough?
47. About the Word
48. Refined by Fire
49. Beautiful, Magnificent
50. I've Heard it Said
51. Prayer for You
52. All the Riches
53. Sweetly Boundless
54. Farewell
55. Time for Good Cheer
56. Hard Side of Heaven
57. Run Away
58. Sleep Softly
59. Keep Dreaming
60. Happy Birthday Anyway
61. Mere Mortals
62. Cricket's Destiny

63. Soldiers Make Good Promises
64. Good and Better
65. Dancing by the Sea
66. Somewhere a Song Plays
67. Distant Dreams
68. Tell Me Your Story
69. The World is You
70. This Promise is Forever
71. Hero of My Dreams
72. In My Dream
73. You Haunt My Dreams
74. Pain I Cannot Ease
75. Fount of Life
76. Song of the Dead
77. Gift of Time with Her
78. The Teardrop
79. Good Morning
80. Healer's Love
81. Love Shall Find
82. Best Way to Say Goodbye

1. Thin Black Road

There's a thin black road
I have traveled many times.
It leads to peace
In so many ways.
It's kind of hard to describe
For the road's oft unclear.
It unfolds to me
Like a lovely gift
One word at a time.
Then, music fills in the gaps,
Making worries fade away,
As unexplainable peace pours in.
There's a thin black road
It leads me to peace.
When good or ill tidings come
To threaten my equilibrium,
I will travel that road
And return to peaceful calm.

2. Burden Not Seen

Here is the anthem of my soul:
Only the Lord can make me whole.

God, I am asking you to set me free.
I have a burden others cannot see.

I have a need to help out somewhere,
But I need you to take me there.

Lift me up with Holy hands.
Help me pull others from sinking sands.

Give me all the right words to say,
And all this, in your name I'll pray.

For I have a burden others cannot see,
And only you, O Lord, can set me free.

3. To My Former Master

Dear Former Master, listen well,
I am no longer bound for Hell.
Can you not see?
You have no power over me!

I have a new owner,
Christ Jesus, the atoner.
Now, my soul belongs to God.
My path is the one that Jesus trod.

There will be times that I fail.
My feet will surely leave the trail.
But I know I'll never turn back,
No matter how hard you attack.

Your power is truly gone …
As surely as break of dawn,
After an awful, stormy night,
When no hope seems in sight.

4. Not What I'd Pictured

It's not exactly what I'd hoped for,
Not exactly what I'd planned,
Not exactly what I'd pictured in my mind …
When I said, Lord I resign.
Take my life in your hands,
Lead me on to the Promised Lands.

It's not exactly what I'd hoped for,
Not exactly what I'd planned,
Not exactly what I'd pictured in my mind …
But I like it anyway.
No more guilt, no more shame.
No more shifting around blame.

It's not exactly what I'd hoped for,
Not exactly what I'd planned,
Not exactly what I'd pictured in my mind …
But the peace of mind is worth it.
Jesus Christ, in my life
Helps me work through grief and strife.

5. Why the Tears?

Why the tears?
When no one's around
To hear you cry …
Why the tears?

Why the tears?
When you know in your heart
That the Lord is near …
Why the tears?

Dry those tears.
And remember the Lord
Is always there.
Dry those tears.

Dry those tears.
And lean on the promises
Of the King.
Dry those tears.

6. Speak Soft Words
(Also in *Heartfelt Cases 1: The Collins Case*)

So, here I am again,
Baffled and confused,
Come before you, Lord God.
Saying …
Please give me wisdom.
Please give me wisdom.
For my head is pounding
With the problems of the world around me.
Won't you, please give me wisdom.
Won't you, lead my heart today, Lord.

So, here I am again,
Worn and weary,
Come before you, Lord God.
Saying …
Speak soft words to me, Lord.
Speak soft words to me.
For my ears are ringing
With the loud shouts of the world around me.
Won't you, speak soft words to me, Lord.
Won't you speak soft words today.

Totally at peace.
That is where I'll be
When the Lord God is near.

7. My Days are Numbered
(Also in *Heartfelt Cases 2: The Kiverson Case*)

My days are numbered,
And I don't know that number.
But I thank God for every breath I take,
For every moment He's seen fit to grant me.
This I do know: I'm in good hands.

My days are numbered,
And I don't know that number.
But I thank my God for every day
Of this life, I oft take for granted.
This I do know: I'm in good hands.

My days are numbered,
And I don't know that number.
But I know God knows,
And that's a comfort in trying times.
This I do know: I'm in good hands.

8. No Sleep

Why can't I sleep tonight?
You'd think I'd never thought a single thought
And had to make up for it all tonight.
Why can't I sleep tonight?

I cannot sleep tonight.
My mind is racing to a land of dreams.
It races to a world full of worries.
I cannot sleep tonight.

Lord, help me sleep tonight.
For only You can Solve my problems,
Only You can set my mind at ease.
Lord, help me sleep tonight.

9. Times of Trouble
(Also in *Heartfelt Cases 3: The Davidson Case*)

So, it seems like your world
Is falling apart all around you.
Tell me, what will you do?
Where will you go?
And who can you turn to in times of trouble?

There are several ways to answer all these.
The best thing to do in times of need
Is to fall to your knees,
For the best place to be when you can't go on,
Is in the arms of your Heavenly Father.

So, it seems like your world
Is falling apart all around you.
Tell me, what will you do?
Where will you go?
And who can you turn to in times of trouble?

God's the only one who can make you strong
Enough to stand against the world.
With His holy help,
You will make it through each fiery trial,
With your heart and mind yet whole.

So, when it seems like your world
Is falling apart all around you.
I say, fall to your knees
And seek out the Lord,
And he will help you in times of trouble.

Thin Black Road

10. Is There Anything ...

I want to shout to all the world
That God is the Lord over all.
I want ask them all this:
Is there anything more beautiful
Than the sight of a star-studded night
That heralds to all the world,
Just how much God cares for the details?

I know that things go wrong,
But God is always there.
I want to ask you one more thing:
Is there anything more wonderful
Than the peace of mind that comes
From knowing God knows
Everything that goes on around you?

Thin Black Road

11. Walk On

There is peace in my life.
There is hope in my life.
There is joy in my life.
There is strength in my life because …
God has given me peace.
God has given me hope.
God has given me joy.
God has given me strength to walk on.

In the strength of the Lord,
I will walk on through trials,
I will walk on through pain,
I will walk on through whatever comes my way.

Long ago, God did say,
When you're weak then you're strong.
When is seems like you can't go on,
Call on God and you will
Always find strength to walk on.

In the strength of the Lord,
You will walk on through trials,
You will walk on through pain,
You will walk on through whatever comes your way.

12. God Will have the Last Word
(Also in *Heartfelt Cases 1: The Collins Case*)

As the world falls apart me around me,
I think of this truth and peace comes:
God will have the last word.
He has in ages past, He still does today,
And the future's certain when it comes to this:
God will have the last word.
Our Mighty King came to Earth
As a baby, to live and love and die,
But that wasn't the end by far,
Jesus had the last word when He rose again!

13. Beautiful Day

The beauty of this day is not lost on me.
The sun is shining brightly.
The sky is a pretty shade of blue,
And there are fluffy little white clouds
Soaring on the wings of the same wind
That plays with my hair.
O the care, O the detail, O the thought
That went into designing this world!
It's a humbling, comforting thought to see
That God's so much bigger than me.

I know I have much to do today,
But I can't help but stop
I can't help but stop and enjoy,
The beauty of the world around me.
A thousand dreary days are worth it to
Enjoy the full measure of the beauty of this day.
O the care, O the detail, O the thought
That went into designing this world!
It's a humbling, comforting thought to see
That God's so much bigger than me.

There's a sense of peace that comes
And surrounds my heart when I realize that
The same God who created that sun,
The same God who painted that sky,
The same God who designed those clouds,
Is the same God who rules my life.
O the care, O the detail, O the thought
That went into designing me!
It's a humbling, comforting thought to see
That God's so much bigger than me.
O, the beauty of this day is not lost on me.

14. Deep-seated Peace

There may not be overflowing joy
Coming out of me but I know
There's a deep-seated peace hiding in me.
Look deep in my eyes.
Can you see the deep-seated peace hiding in me?
What's that?
You say you can't see the peace ...
Oh well,
I know there's a deep-seated peace hiding in me.
It flows from the fountain of life
That sprang up when I accepted Christ.
So though you may not see
The deep-seated peace hiding in me,
All can see the source of that peace.
It is Christ the Lord who reigns on high.
So come and accept him and receive
The deep-seated peace hiding in me.

15. Am I Hiding My Heart?

When you look at me what do you see?
Do you see a fire to serve the Lord?
Or am I hiding my heart deep inside?

Every good thing comes from the Lord my God.
I am so blessed, but how can I share,
The many good things God has given to me?
From this day on, I will walk by faith,
Trusting that I am under grace.

When you look at me what do you see?
Do you see a fire to serve the Lord?
Or am I hiding my heart deep inside?

Do you know the things that haunt my dreams?
I fear to fail, I fear to fall,
But most of all, I fear I fail to do.
My own salvation's not the issue here.
What is, is that I'm here and the lost are there.

When you look at me what do you see?
Do you see a fire to serve the Lord?
Or am I hiding my heart deep inside?

16. Rain Down Wisdom

I wish I were perfect,
But I know that cannot be
This side of Heaven.
So here I am, my Father,
On my knees, begging you please
Rain down wisdom on me.

O I know my salvation's sure,
From the very day I surrendered.
In You, I know, I am strong,
But there are times when I am so weak
Deep down inside of me.
So here I am, my Father,
On my knees, begging you please
Rain down wisdom on me.

The many sides of me are at war
Trying to grab pieces of my heart.
Lord, I meant what I said, when I said,
"My heart is yours."
So won't you please
Rain down wisdom on me.

Teach me how to be a servant.
Teach me how to be a friend.
Teach me how to praise you properly.
Here I am, Father,
On my knees, begging you please
Rain down wisdom on me.

17. Every Moment

Every moment is a gift,
Though it may not seem that way.
Even trials have their place
As they teach us to pray:
"Father God, rain down peace over me
For I am struggling through life today."

Every moment is a gift,
Though it may not seem that way.
Think of all the good things in your life.
Have you neglected to say:
"Father God, thank you for blessing me
All of these days and in all of these ways …"?

Every moment is a gift,
Though it may not seem that way.
So cherish every moment
And continue to pray:
"Father God, teach me to follow your ways
For I am your servant all of my days."

18. Worry Won't Win Any Wars

It seems like this life is one tiny war after another.
Whether they be mental, spiritual, physical, emotional,
At some point you're gonna have to fight them.

What weighs heavily upon your mind?
Are you worried that you can't pay your bills?
Are you worried that you can't feed your kids?
Are you worried that that person close to you
Doesn't seem to love you?
Are you worried?
Do not worry,
For worry won't win any wars right now.

What weighs heavily upon your mind?
Are you worried 'cause you just failed that test?
Are you worried 'cause you haven't got a job?
Are you worried 'cause your best friend's father died
And you just don't know what to say?
Are you worried?
Do not worry,
For worry won't win any wars right now.

When you get a free moment open a Bible
Find your strength in the written word.
As for the spiritual war raging around us,
The weapons to win this war were given to us long ago.
When you get a free moment open a Bible
Find your answers in the written word.
Though worry won't win any wars right now,
We have a heavenly Father who cares.
So when you get a free moment open a Bible
And find your peace in the written word.

19. Driving Me Crazy

Worry is driving me a little bit crazy.
Maybe I spoke too hastily,
Maybe I didn't think this through …
No, I know I didn't think this through.
So what am I gonna do?
'Cause worry is driving me a little bit crazy.

O I know it won't do any good.
But I cannot help it
'Cause it just plain comes.
O I know God's got it all in hand,
And I know that things will be all right.
But worry's still driving me a little bit crazy.

Lord, come and be my help tonight.
Come and be my peace of mind.
Come and be my sanity …
'Cause worry is driving me a little bit crazy.

20. Freely

Freely ye have received the good news
That Jesus came to save all this world.
So freely give to those around you,
The hope that you have hiding inside.
Declare everywhere who you are,
A son or daughter of the one King,
The High King of Heaven.

Fear not what they may think
For they must hear that God loves them.
No one will ever escape from the truth
That all will perish without the Lord.
But there is hope in our Holy Father,
The one King, the High King, God in Heaven.

Freely ye have received this good news
So freely give to all those around you.
There are so many in this world who are hurting.
Tell them by speaking, show them by doing.
Let them see Christ shining.
Let them see how wonderful it is to truly be free.

21. Listen

Do I speak too much?
Should I pray more?
Should I listen more?
All too often I am too busy
Crying out, "O God hear my plea …"
That I'm not listening for His answer.
Then, I wonder why I receive no reply,
When I'm not listening
'Cause I'm too busy complaining
Of all the things that befall me.

O Father, speak to me tonight.
I've come to listen to You.
Come and teach me the meaning
Of a quiet time with You.
Come and teach my heart to listen.
For long ago, I mastered the art
Of telling You every problem on my mind,
But I forgot to listen.
So teach me how to listen …
For Your words of comfort and wisdom.

22. Better

What makes the life of a Christian any better?
Are we better than anybody else?
Not by a long shot, not even close.
No one is better than anybody else,
And no one will ever be good enough.
Hence, the reason for the grace of God.
Hence, the reason for Christ's sacrifice
At the cross to redeem this fallen world.

What makes the life of a Christian any better?
Are we better off than anybody else?
Yes, we are better off than all those
Who do not have the Lord
To lean on in times of trouble.
For though today may be hard,
We can know that tomorrow will be better,
And even if it's not, we can still rejoice.
For hard times will only make it
That much sweeter when our broken hearts
Finally make it to Heaven's perfect peace.

23. Dancing Sun

See the sun dance with joy.
Yesterday, and the day before, it rained,
Making it hard to see beauty all around.
But today the clouds have run,
Revealing a clear blue sky.
See the sun shining forth,
Bouncing to and fro off everything,
O it's quite a sight!

Everything revealed by light looks better.
See the sun; it dances there
Making things look happier.
Come take a walk with me,
And we'll watch the sun dance.

Just as things look better by light,
So God's love shining through
Reveals the best inside of you.
Let God's love shine through
So they may see what they could have.
Invite them all to take a walk
To see the dancing sun.
Then, share the Kingdom of the Son.
Some will see the truth and be saved.

Everything revealed by light looks better.
See the sun; it dances there
Making things look happier.
Come take a walk with me,
And we'll watch the sun dance.

Thin Black Road

24. Made to Praise

As I walked around on this gorgeous day,
I reflected on my life and then prayed,
"Father God, thank you for being You.
Thank you too for the many blessings …
I would try to count them,
But they are countless.
Thank you for being holy …
All good things in life reflect You …"

At that moment I realized …
You and I, we were made
To praise His name.
You and I, we were made
To love and be loved.
You and I, we were made
To live, learn, grow, and pray.
You and I, we were made
To lift our hands, bow our hearts,
And open our eyes to the truth.
We were made to praise the Lord!
We were made to praise Him!

25. Peace of God

Peace of God reign in me
Help me see Your glory.
It's like a crown to be found
On everything around,
But I cannot see it today!

Peace of God reign in me
Help me see Your glory.
For only You are Lord Most High.
Only You can satisfy
Every desire of my heart.

Peace of God reign in me
Help me see Your glory.
For I am scared of today,
And what tomorrow may bring my way.
Wrap me in Your peace.

Peace of God reign in me
Help me see Your glory.
For only with my eyes on You
Will I be brought through
Every trial I must face.

Peace of God reign in me
Help me see Your glory.
For only You can give me peace
May I never ever cease
Praising Your holy name!

26. Right Place to Sing

I sing in the shower, don't you?
I sing in the car, don't you?
I sing on the way to class, don't you?
I sing almost anywhere
For almost anywhere is the
Right place to sing
Praises to the King.

I sing as I take a walk.
I sing as I stand in line.
I sing in the grocery store.
I sing almost anywhere
For almost anywhere is the
Right place to sing
Praises to the King.

I do get a few strange looks,
But I don't really care,
I say, "Let them stare …"
All they'll see is me
Singing praises to my King.
I am practicing for Heaven
Where everywhere will be the
Right place to sing
Praises to the King!

27. Light in My Eyes

Let there always be a light in my eyes
For it speaks of love for this life.
I am eager to learn the things
God has in store for me.
Though things may change,
For now I am at peace.

Let there always be a light in my eyes
For it reflects God's Word in me.
All good things come from God's hands.
Though evil abounds all around
We can know God's promise
To set things right in the end.

Let there always be a light in my eyes
For it shows the hope within.
As long as the Light lives in me,
I live in the Light
And the Light dispels all darkness.
I will find peace in the Light.

28. We Needed a Hero

We needed a hero
And God provided well.
Though I can barely fathom it,
I sure do believe:
The wrath of God has no remedy.
The grace of God knows no bounds.
How can this be?

We needed a hero
And God provided well.
I have felt the grace of God.
And the Bible is filled
With tales of wrath.
Yet with tales of wrath
Come tales of grace.

There is no greater tale
Than the true account of Jesus's life.
We needed a hero
And God provided well.

29. Chosen One

I know the Chosen One.
He is my friend.
Let me tell you all about Him.
He is holy, mighty, just,
Wonderful in every way.
He is loving, kind, gentle,
And powerful in every way.

I know the Chosen One.
He is my friend.
I'm going to praise His name!
He is the Counselor, Prince of Peace,
Lord over all things.
He is the Shepherd, perfect Judge,
And Defender of all.

I know the Chosen One.
He is my friend.
I will strive to be like Him.
He has mastered all things admirable,
And saved the lives of many.
He is the Chosen One;
I am a messenger.
Let us strive to be like Him!

30. Move, Mountain, Move

So long I've gone this journey
Walking in a land full of lost.
I see their pain clear as day
And I have the soothing answer.
Wish that they would know my Lord.
Such would be sweet to my soul.
He is peace brought to life.
He sought not His will but
Submitted to death for all.
My soul weeps at the word of the Lord
"All fall short of the glory of God."
And again, I weep, this time for joy,
Knowing God sent Christ for you and me.
It seems so long since I last spoke
On behalf of those like me.
They are stubborn in heart,
Solid as mountains set in their ways.
God's been known to shake the earth
To move a mountain where He pleases.
I would not wish ill on anyone,
But if it saves their soul,
Maybe shaking's the way to go.
I have faith so I'll say,
"Move, Mountain, move!"

31. End and Beginning

End of a day, beginning of a new
Here I am trying to think.
Some profound thought lies
On the edge of my imagination.
I can almost feel it.
Something weighs on my heart.
It feels like it was made of lead.
Lord, move heart and mind.
Bring me to the point where I can say
"I picked up my cross today,
And I was glad."
Many times, I carry on Christian duty,
Looking like somebody just died.
I contemplate good acts,
Sigh, and think, "I suppose I'll help
For it's what Christ would do."
Well, it's a good thing God forgives
And uses us despite false motives!
I cried out and my eyes were opened.
It's the end of a day, beginning of a new …

32. Best Day

There's a gray cast to the sky today.
Rain hangs in the air like a mystery.
Will it come today or tomorrow?
Does it matter either way?
All things happen in God's time.
Impatient as I am, the days slip by
And I can't reclaim a one.
These are the best days of life they say,
But I'm starting to see
Every day in God's arms,
Learning from the Holy One,
Is the best day of my life.
How humbling, how amazing to know
God knows each small flame.
I am one in ten trillion
How can it be that God knows me?
Such a thing lies far beyond my thoughts,
But He's good and I know He knows
Everything that shall come to pass.
Won't you come and join this family.
Then today and every day, good or ill,
Will be the best day of your life!

33. Let Him In

There's a stranger knocking at your door.
Don't be scared; don't be shy.
Open that door; let Him in.
He's the most patient man there ever was.
He won't shout; He won't curse
But he just might cry.
After all, it's for you He sacrificed.
He's not going away; let Him in.
You can drown the knock with noise.
You can stand behind the barricades.
You can huddle down and close your eyes.
But you can't wait forever,
For you might not have that time.
Just try to face the fact:
He's not going away.
Let Him in.

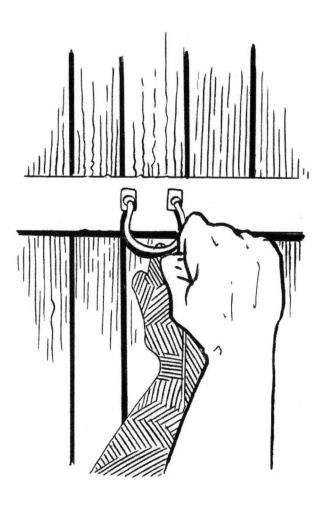

34. Dance to Life

I've got a tune in my head,
Slippery as a ball of grease.
Can't keep track of it.
It goes where it wants to.
High or low or somewhere in between.
I remember now, but wait a moment
I'll probably lose it just like before.

It's kind of bouncy.
Dang, I'll be up tonight.
I feel like dancing.
Won't you dance with me?
What shall we dance to?
How about life?

35. The Long Story

The past is the past and unchangeable.
The future is there to be redefined.
I suppose you could say,
"Every day was written long ago,
So why try to change?"

Life may be one long story,
Part comedy, part tragedy,
But the way this script was written
We have a choice to be
Hero, villain, or victim.
At times, we play all three.
We cannot control much,
But that's the adventure.

Heroes are made every day.
Until they breathe their last,
Anyone can change.
What's holding you back?
Everyone has their trials.
Heroes simply rise above.
How will your story end?

36. Never Alone

The loss is deep; the pain is sharp.
You cry out into dark
"Nobody knows my pain!"
Hate to contradict the hurt,
But you're not alone out here.
When darkness falls and all seems lost
Turn to the Holy One.
Cry upon God above.
He's the only one who can
Take that pain and fling it far,
Pour soothing peace until you rest.
Best of all, He loves you.
He died to rise and conquer sin.
Though we still feel its blow,
We can always know He knows.
He will walk each hard step.
He will share in love and pain.
You are never alone.

37. Somewhere Today

Somewhere today somebody died.
Maybe he was a soldier carrying out his duty.
Maybe she was a child succumbing to disease.
Maybe he thought nobody cared,
So he took his own life.
Maybe she was a mommy
Somebody's gonna miss.
Somewhere today somebody died,
And somewhere today somebody's crying,
"Is this all there is to life,
A series of steps towards a hungry grave?"
I refuse to believe that this is all.
I have seen and heard too many miracles.
Every discovery, self-revelation, and peaceful
Moment is a gift from God
Who is just and full of grace.
We are weak and prone to fail,
But somewhere today somebody's learning.
Maybe he took his first step.
Maybe she passed that tough test.
Maybe he saw how she loves him.
Maybe somewhere today somebody
Finally surrendered their life to God.
Maybe somewhere today somebody's finally living.

38. Grim Day

This day didn't start so well,
Pouring rain and looking o so grim.
Had to remind myself God promised
Not to drown the world again.
Still no sun to be found here, but
At least the clouds are much less menacing.
I'd say consider each raindrop
Isn't it neat, but then
I'd just be lying to you.
Ever notice we have a tendency
To focus on irrelevant things?
People die every day
Never knowing Christ saves.
They had their chance to make a choice.
Do not miss yours too.
If you know the King then declare it.
There's nothing to fear.
Though this day didn't start out so well,
It turned out all right.
Life is full of storms,
But my God is full of grace.

39. Lost Ones

Are you a lost one?
I know that sounds strange,
But are you a lost one?
My Master sent me out on a journey
To find all the lost ones
Who knew not the way.
Are you a lost one?
Are you waiting for someone
To find you out here alone in this cold?
Are you a lost one?
Well, no matter, I've found you at last.
Come with me we'll have a party.

Won't you come home with me?
Don't you see?
The Master's arms are always
Open to the lost ones.
That is, you and me, we're one family.
Once torn apart by sin and shame,
Now united through Christ.
Won't you celebrate with me?
We're lost no more!
Praise the Lord God,
We're lost no more!

40. New Title

God walk with me on this journey,
For I know not the way to go.
As you guide me, I will conquer
Doubt, fear, despair, and pain.
Though this world may be fallen,
Your beauty shines everywhere.
Stars that shine only at night,
Newborn babies sleeping softly,
Trees clothed in leaves and light,
All declare You are here.
God You reign forevermore.
Thank you for this life.
Thank you for being holy.
All that power, all that glory,
All cast down to save the lost.
Chief of sinners once my title,
Stripped away by saving grace,
Slave to sin or servant of God,
I have chosen my place.
I'll declare it out loud.
My new title: child of God.

41. Money Can and Cannot

Money cannot buy peace of mind.
Money cannot buy happiness.
Money cannot buy lasting love.
Well, what good is it?

The quest for money has claimed many lives.
Abuse and hate have claimed many more.
Universal goals of love and peace
Get forgotten when money is at stake.
The rich and famous may live all right,
But thousands die every day from poverty.
Can money solve this problem?

Money may ransom a rich man's life,
But it put him in danger in the first place.
Money may buy a short-term cure,
But will it save your soul?
Money may buy food for a day.
By tomorrow you'll be hungry.

Money cannot buy peace of mind.
Money cannot buy happiness.
Money cannot buy lasting love.
Is it worth dying for?

42. God Doesn't Know How to Fail

Went to church just the other day.
Heard Joseph's tale told in a new way.
Heard how he was sold as a slave,
Wrongly accused, thrown into jail,
Forgotten by so many people
For so many years,
But not forgotten by God.
My God who doesn't know how to fail.

Wondered how this message applied to me.
Kept returning to this one point.
My God doesn't know how to fail.
I'm sure I fail many times,
Complain endlessly, fall on my face,
But I can always be sure
My God doesn't know how to fail.

43. Enemy

How many times have you heard the devil say,
"I'm not the enemy.
You won't get rid of me.
I'm not your enemy!
I have only your interests in mind."?

How many times have you echoed in your heart,
"I'm not the enemy.
Though evil surround me,
I will not be consumed.
I have only good in mind."?

When did you become an expert
At lying to yourself?
Don't you realize
You have become the enemy?
Evil has swallowed you whole.

Come back from darkness!
No evil is too great.
It is still not too late.
Turn from this destructive path
Or become your own worst enemy.

44. When You're Weary

When you're weary, when you're worried,
When this world's got you so low
The earth would have to open
To let you sink lower,
That's when you know for sure
You need Christ in your life.
Why wait 'til trouble comes?
Why wait 'til the ache in your heart gets
So bad you think it might just burst open wide
And scatter small pieces from shore to shore?

When you're weary, when you're worried,
Cry out to the Lord.
He will hear you. He will answer.
He will give you peace of mind.
Things still might not go right,
But you can know for sure
God will always be waiting
To catch your tears.
In Him, find rest, weary one.

45. Mountain of Troubles

There may be a mountain of troubles ahead,
But always remember you're never alone.
When you need strength look back and see
The many miracles manifest in thee.
God is forever gracious and true.
He will lead you day by day.
Take life one day at a time.
Tomorrow's got its own troubles.
No use borrowing more today.
Let His peace reign in you.
Then, no mountain of troubles
Can weigh your heart down.
There may be a mountain of troubles ahead,
But the Rock behind you is far greater.

46. Had Enough?

When nothing goes right and you feel so lost,
When everything's right and you still feel lost,
Ask yourself some questions.

Have you had enough?
Have you had enough of running your life?
Have you had enough of making mistakes?
Have you had enough of feeling lost?
Have you had enough?

Don't you think it's time you surrendered it all?
Don't you think it's time to say,
"God, I've had enough!
Take my life and make me more like You."

I'm not saying lightning's going to fall from the sky,
God's going to speak from the mountains,
Or anything of that nature,
But it's never happened in the course of history
Someone cried out, "Lord, help me!"
And didn't receive an answer.
Have you had enough?

47. About the Word

You'd think I'd know
My own heart by now,
But it confuses me every day.
Have I forgotten what it's like
To be a sinner under grace?
Have I forgotten how to ask
The Lord for daily wisdom?

Some songs make no sense to me.
When I pause to reflect,
I come to realize
Sometimes I think too hard.
It's not about the song at all.
It's about the Word and
The Word made flesh and
The Flesh that died and
The Man that rose again!
It's about the Word.

48. Refined by Fire

When it seems everything is going wrong,
Just hold on to this thought.
Every trial and tribulation
Is only a spark,
Merely a part of cleansing fire.
Refined by fire.
That's what I'll be.
If this trial don't break me,
It will make me into something better
Than I had ever imagined.

Out of this fire I'll walk unscathed
For fire can burn me, maybe break me,
But it can never take me away from God.
He's my comfort, my great provider.
When this world weighs on my heart,
I'll just try to remember
It's only a part of refining fire.
This trial can never break me long.
It can only make me stronger
By driving me closer to God.

49. Beautiful, Magnificent

In ancient days, they looked
At the moon and stars,
Saw how beautiful, saw how magnificent,
And called them god.
I look at the moon and stars
See how beautiful, see how magnificent
And say, "Praise the Lord!
That sight is no accident.
All that is beautiful, all that is perfect
Is crafted by God."

All hail King Jesus!
He made the moon and stars.
He made you and me.
He made us truly free.
Can't help but stand and sing
All hail King Jesus!
He is beautiful, most magnificent,
And He is my God!

50. I've Heard it Said

About this time, I always think of my life.
Try to reconcile what I've done and will do.
There are several goals I have in mind.
I wonder if they're all my own.
I've heard it said, "You can't lose salvation."
Don't know if I believe my ears.
I've heard it said, "You can't lose salvation,"
But I know it's true
You can fall away from right.
Don't think I'm in much danger of that,
And that's probably where the trouble starts.
I've heard it said, "You can't lose salvation."
That may be true but you can sure fall far.
Falling may be the best thing,
But it sure ain't easy on the way down!
I've asked God to mold me like clay,
Then it crossed my mind:
Molding may be the best thing,
But sometimes it hurts like crazy.
I've heard it said, "You can't lose salvation."
True or not, I'll not lose mine.
Though the molding may break me,
I'll be better for the change.

51. Prayer for You

Heard you were down today.
Didn't know what to say,
So I started to pray.

God, you know my heart
And that I don't have words to start.
Please be with my friend.
Wrap your peace around her mind.
Help her with answers she seeks to find.
Let her know
Every pain helps us grow.
Life can seem without direction
Walking forth waiting for correction,
But you're no stranger to rejection.
Give her the strength to carry
Your love to those you would marry
Your heart to and call heirs
To your kingdom. Nothing else compares.

I found words to say
When I began to pray
May God work in your heart today.

52. All the Riches

Seeped in a world where everything
Can be bought or bartered for,
I'm amazed every time I realize anew:
All the riches of all the ages
Cannot purchase the freedom
I have so freely in Christ alone.
Freedom from thoughts and worries.
Freedom from tempting sins.
Shackles I had felt and never felt
Fell away one day,
And no matter how many times
I try to climb back into them
They will hold me no more.
All my money and other riches
Could not accomplish what one
Man's perfect life and death did.
All the riches of all the ages
Cannot purchase the freedom
I have so freely in Christ alone.

53. Sweetly Boundless

Like the oceans,
Clear night skies,
Thoughts that lay behind
Stormy eyes,
True love is sweetly boundless.
Some would take that to mean
Any one of a thousand things.
All I meant by what I said:
Truest love there ever was belonged to God.
Though I wander far away from the truth,
True love pursues my soul.
Some would call it foolishness.
Others would agree with me:
Love that would not spare the Son
Can only be seen as sweetly boundless.
All other loves fade with time.
Not my Jesus.
He's forever,
For His love is sweetly boundless.

54. Farewell

I was pondering how
To best say goodbye
When it crossed my mind
It's not really goodbye.
It's more like farewell
As in fare ye well for I might
Not see you for a long time,
Maybe not 'til the end of this age.
But if you know God
And I do too
And we both trust in Christ
To be our perfect sacrifice
There is no goodbye, only farewell
As in fare ye well for I might
Not see you for a long time.
So walk with God
And I will too
And when we meet again
We can share our many tales
Until then fare ye well.

55. Time for Good Cheer

Christmas comes but once a year.
O, what a time for good cheer.
Yet here we are running around,
Going half-crazy buying just one more thing.
We slap on a smile but complain inside.
"It's freezing cold and there's no sign of snow."
"The tree fell over twice ..."
In the midst of the chaos
I must pause or lose my mind.
I try to remember.
Christmas comes but once a year.
It should be a time for good cheer.
The reason for this whole season is
Jesus Christ who gave up Heaven to
Ransom sinners from the fires of hell!
O, what a happy thought that is!
How many times have I given thanks
For such a priceless gift?
Christmas may be once a year
But with Christ in me
Every day's a time for good cheer!

56. Hard Side of Heaven

I've shed my share of tears
And I'll probably part with more.
Somewhere in this mess
I will find my peace.

It's always hard to be told
You're not good enough.

Some part of me is crying,
"Who's holding the standard?"
The other part of me knows
It doesn't really matter.
We're on the hard side of Heaven.

This is me broken.
This is me whole.
This is me finding the pieces
Somebody scattered.
This is me finding peace
In the One who crossed on over.
The same One who rules my life.

We may be on the hard side of Heaven.
But my help and hope can be found
In the pages of a Book,
In the God-shaped space in my soul.

57. Run Away

Wait!
Please hear me out!
I see you're running away again.
Though it is breaking me,
I won't stop you long.
Please just answer a few questions.
Is all this running really worth it?
Will the bottle help you understand?
Will the drugs drive away your pain?
I know you miss your father.
I sure do.
War's never easy but neither is life.
Think of all you leave behind
Every time you run away.
I've cried. I've begged. I've prayed
God would give us wisdom.
I have no profound words to say,
Only this promise:
No matter how many times you run away
I'll be waiting here for you.
You'll never cease to be my son.
Just remember God's not like me.
He will chase you. He will find you
No matter how far you run away.
Is all this running really worth it?

58. Sleep Softly

Go to sleep now. Dawn will come soon.
Go to sleep now. I'll be right here.
Go to sleep now. No need to fear.
Night and day, I will pray
One day, you will know the Lord.
One day, you will understand.
One day, you will make a choice.
Night and day, I will pray
You choose to follow God's way.
I wish I could fight your battles.
I wish I could make your choice.
I know I wish in vain.
I can guide you on the way,
But ultimately the choice remains yours.
The grace of God can save you.
One day, you will understand.
Until that day, do not worry.
Do not worry. God will watch you.
Do not worry. God will guide you.
Until that day, sleep softly.
Sleep softly, little one, God is with you.
Sleep softly, little one, God will guide you.
Sleep softly, little one, God loves you.

59. Keep Dreaming

Dreams are born in inspired moments
And last a lifetime.
Dreams lend strength to the hopeless,
Direction to the lost.
When you're weary,
Keep dreaming, keep hoping.
Hope will lead you through to a new day.
Maybe that day will be worse
Than the last one,
But it's a new day,
A day for new dreams,
Dreams with hope enough
To carry you through dark times.
When things get so bad
You think you might just snap in two,
Keep dreaming, keep hoping.
Hope will lend you strength to go on.
You will walk through your trials.
You will make it to a new day.
That new day may see your dreams come true.

60. Happy Birthday Anyway

So, you're one day older.
They say you're one year older.
That makes you sound so old.
Happy birthday anyway.
Don't focus on tomorrow.
Today's your special day.
Tomorrow you'll just be one day older.
Happy birthday anyway.
This year sure did go by.
The next will fly faster.
Take heart. You're aging well.
Happy birthday anyway.

61. Mere Mortals

Come gather around and I'll tell you a tale.
I'll tell you a tale of life,
Tell you a tale of death.
I'll tell you a tale
But the lesson you learn is up to you.

While mere mortals slept out beneath the stars,
Tucked in tiny tents in neat little rows,
The spirits crept between them
And whispered in their ears.
"Dear mortal, I hope you sleep well.
Tomorrow comes far too soon
Bringing war, strife, and death
To friend and foe alike.
The battles rage around you
With Death winning every one.
You never know when the day's dawn
Will be the last dawn you see
So live your life accordingly.
Make calm moments, short letters, sweet smiles
The substance of your dreams.
Sleep well, dear soldier,
Tomorrow comes far too soon
Ye have not long to be a mere mortal."

62. Cricket's Destiny

Once alive
Now no more.
I crossed this earth
Singing summer songs
Softly.

The end came
Swift and sure
Before I had the time
To cry out why.

Wish
I had just
One more moment
To live.

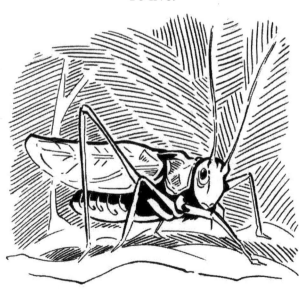

63. Soldiers Make Good Promises

When I heard the news,
I cried out "Why?
Why, O God, let that good man die?
Accidents happen every day,
But why take the father of a little girl
So soon after losing her mother?"

Hardest thing I ever had to do was
Hold that little girl, hear her cry,
Feel her shake, and find the strength to say,
"Dear LeAnn,
It's okay to cry.
You don't know me,
But my name's Jim.
I know you feel all alone.
Come, take my hand.
In your parents' absence,
I'll do my best to raise you well,
Just as I promised I would."

Did your daddy ever tell you
Soldiers make good promises?
Did your daddy ever tell you
That your mommy was a soldier?
Did he ever tell you how
She died for me?
I am quite convinced
She set my soul free.

For some reason far beyond me
She chose to be my friend.

Thin Black Road

I remember the day she died.
Though the sun was blazing,
The desert heat couldn't shake her smile.
The convoy had gone well
Until the shots rang out,
And we got out to fight.
At her orders, grunts like me fell into line.
We fought hard and fared well,
But the enemy had higher ground.

Did your daddy ever tell you
That your mommy was a soldier?
Did he ever tell you how
She set my soul free?

Hunkered down behind a pile of sand,
I found myself next to her.
She flashed a smile and shouted,
"God is in control!"
I replied with something vile.
She just ignored me.
I'll never forget her steady blue eyes
As she calmly replied,
"One day you will believe."

Did your daddy ever tell you
That your mommy was a soldier?
Did he ever tell you how she
Took three bullets for me?

Before I could catch my breath,
A man stood before us, rifle ready.
My hands froze, my shots went wide.

His first bullet grazed my head.
The next three marked for me found her instead.
Now pinned beneath her, I could only watch.
Somewhere she found strength to shoot.
That man never knew what hit him.

Did your daddy ever tell you
That your mommy was a soldier?
Did he ever tell you her
Last words to me concerned you?

With her dying breath, she spoke softly,
"Jim, you will know the Lord.
He has spoken to me.
Tell Tom I love him.
Soon, he will join me.
Take good care of my little girl.
Help her find the way."

That day, I made a promise
To care for you until I die.

Did your daddy ever tell you
That your mommy was a soldier?
Did he ever tell you
Soldiers make good promises?

64. Good and Better

I am well aware I am only one,
But you are one as well.
If you hear this cry for help—
That's good.
If you hear and add your voice—
That's better.
I believe in a land that's greater.
I believe in a time without fear.
I believe you and I can change
This whole world one soul at a time.
I am well aware I am only one,
But you are one as well.
If you and I raise our voices—
That's good.
If someone hears and joins—
That's better.
Our differences may be great,
But I know we both agree on this:
We believe in a time without fear.
We believe in a land where hearts
Are cradled and cherished—not broken.
And we can change this whole world
One soul at a time.

65. Dancing by the Sea

Daddy, do you remember
How it used to be when
There were three in this family?
Sure, we didn't have much,
But we had it all!
We'd save for months and rise at dawn
Just to go dancing by the sea.
Mommy would hold me,
You would hold her, and
With nothing but the sea birds watching,
We'd all go dancing by the sea.
Seems like such a long time
Since I lost you both to one fool
Going the wrong way on a one way.
The bottle won't fix this,
But one thing just might …
Mommy may still be gone,
But the sea's still there
And there are lots more birds to see us.
Can we go dancing by the sea?

66. Somewhere a Song Plays

Somewhere a song plays for you,
Plays for me, plays for what we
Used to be.
I've known no sweeter time
Than the days spent with you,
Learning and living and breathing
Deeply of the peace that indwells you.
Lies came between us
And then a war.
Now I'm not sure of most things,
But one thing I know for sure:
My greatest lie was saying
I held no love for you.
I played the fool, but senses returned
So, I sought you to ask:
Can you hear that sweet melody?
Can that melody mend you and me to we?
Somewhere a song plays for you,
Plays for me, plays for what we
Used to be.

67. Distant Dreams

I am hard pressed to find
A future satisfying to my soul.
Distant dreams lie beyond me
Like a ribbon, bonny blue,
Tied to a far-off signpost.
I can see it waiving gaily,
Drawing my eyes to that sign,
But that cruel sign's many symbols
Refuse to explain my dreams.
As I draw ever nearer,
Seems that message is never clearer.
Distant dreams lie beyond me
Like a ribbon, bonny blue
Tied to a far-off signpost.
Am I doomed to forever follow
These distant dreams?

68. Tell Me Your Story

Behind every young man or woman
Lies a story waiting to be told.
Tell me your story.
Where did you come from?
What have you experienced?
Where are you going?
These are some of life's
Big questions.
Funny how it's easy to not see
How amazing life can truly be.
So, tell me your story.
What makes you smile?
What makes you laugh or cry?
What do you fear most of all?
Who are you trying to please?
What are your life goals?
Whatever your story may be
There is much more to tell.
So, tell me your story thus far.
Maybe we'll write something new.

69. The World is You

If you wish to kill me, walk away swiftly,
For my whole world is you.
The fire in every star
Cannot compare to you.
The light of life shines so bright
The rocks near come to life.
Don't you know, the world is you?

If you wish to kill me, walk away swiftly,
For my whole world is you.
See and hear the angels sing
They will tell you sweetly
All the gods bound to good
Are manifest in you.
Don't you know, the world is you?

If you wish to kill me, walk away swiftly,
For my whole world is you.
I could be blind and deaf
Yet still feel the good in you.
You haunt my dreams and my heart.
Please tell me we'll never part.
Don't you know, the world is you?

70. This Promise is Forever

At nighttime and all times,
My thoughts dwell with you.
Tell me you'll love me forever.
I could not take a parting, now or ever.
It would break my heart completely,
Shatter my mind, and turn my soul dark.

I am yours; you are mine.
This promise is forever.

You hold my heart in your hands
As you hold my soul with your smile.
Your eyes speak your mind and heart,
But I need to hear the words again.
Tell me you'll love me forever.
Then come what may, life will be perfect.

I am yours; you are mine.
This promise is forever.

I finally found what it means to love
Someone so much it hurts
At the thought of an end.
Tell me you'll love me forever.
I'll be all right though trials or pain
As long as I know I have you.

I am yours; you are mine.
This promise is forever.

Julie C. Gilbert

71. Hero of My Dreams

You're the hero of my dreams,
But you're a stranger.
You're the hero of my dreams,
But I know you through legends alone.
Savior of Calveron, Red Knight,
Lousy Husband, Absent Father,
Hero to all but family.

You're the hero of my dreams,
But I know nothing of the real you.
I'm told I share your blood,
Fiery hair, and fearsome temper.
I know we both loved
The kindest woman who ever walked here.
I know you didn't kill her,
But you might as well have.
You gave her me, then broke her heart
To save some foreign city.

I'm told our sacrifice means something,
But I can't fathom what.
How can you be the hero of my dreams
When my soul only cries, "Villain"?

72. In My Dream

I saw you in a dream.
I saw you sitting here beside me,
Whispering all the good things life can offer.
It wasn't you as you are.
It wasn't you as you used to be.
There was something strange and wonderful
About this new you.

I saw you in a dream.
I saw you standing here before me,
Ice clinging to your heart and soul.
Something about the sight of broken me
Melted the ice and set you free.

I saw you in a dream.
I saw you standing here before me,
Hiding in the shadows,
Caught between desire and uncertainty,
Radiating pain and pleasure,
Wondering how you could comfort me.

I saw you in a dream.
I saw you sitting here beside me,
Whispering all the good things life can offer.
It wasn't you as you are.
It wasn't you as you used to be.
There was something strange and wonderful
About this new you.

In my dream, I beckoned.
It was more like a plea.

In my dream, you rushed forward.
In my dream, you dropped to your knees,
Took me by the hand, lifted my chin,
And wiped away the tears
With naught but a thumb and a grin.
In that moment, all the troubles of the past,
All I see in the future faded,
And I felt safe and whole again.

73. You Haunt My Dreams

Would you believe me if I told you
I cannot tell you how much I love you?
My heart, mind, and soul belong to you.
You cause me pain. You cause me joy.
You haunt my dreams, night or day.

No matter how long I know you,
I'm always learning something new.
Your eyes tell a story I want to hear,
And beg me to tell mine without fear.
Every moment spent apart
Breaks off a piece of my heart.

If I searched this whole world over,
I could not a find a love quite like you.
You make me feel safe, loved, and cherished.
Come and dance with me. Forget your worry.
Tonight belongs to you and me.

Would you believe me if I told you
I cannot tell you how much I love you?
My heart, mind, and soul belong to you.
You cause me pain. You cause me joy.
You haunt my dreams, night or day.

74. Pain I Cannot Ease

It is true.
Life is hard.
No doubts there.
Pain in me I can release.
Pain I see yet cannot touch
Weighs upon my heart.

It's not easy to feel pain.
Worse by far in some ways
Is watching one I love suffer
Pain I cannot ease.

Lord, please hear my heart's cry:
Let me not fail again.
My strength is not enough.
I need You to work in me
Miracles of small moments.

I'm not used to helplessness.
Give me grace to face each day.
Let Your love shine in me.

All these pains I cannot ease
Let me know I'm not perfect,
So, let me be more like You.

75. Fount of Life

The sun fades with flames,
Bright as a new day,
Promise of things to come.
There's sadness and hope here,
Feeling the fire slowly slip away.

What shall I do now?
Where shall I go now?
These echoes remain from many prayers.
Each foray out on my own
Ends in disaster, swift and sure.
There's sadness and hope here,
Feeling the fire slowly slip away.

Come, dear Father, friend of my soul,
Come hold me as I slowly die.
May death to myself and selfish desires
Bring new life like dawn.
May hope spring forth, bright and clear,
For herein lies the fount of life.
There's sadness and hope here,
Feeling the fire slowly slip away.

76. Song of the Dead

Here we are once again,
Singing for the dead.
Here we are once again,
Lamenting life lost.
May this song carry
The dead up to rest.
May it be that when we fall
Someone will sing over our grave.
May it be that when we fall
Someone will carry us on wings
Made of sweet songs.
Then life will go on.

77. Gift of Time with Her

Last night, I dreamed of you.
That's not unusual,
But in this dream I saw
All the stars above.
They were frantic with worry,
Thinking they'd lost one of their own.

I said, "She's with me,
Safe in my arms,
And I'll praise all the heavens
For the gift of time with her.
She's more beautiful than life itself.
The peace I see as she sleeps
Slips softly over me.
I will raise her to know
That the place she left behind
Remembers her fondly,
And we who see her as she is
Will praise all the heavens
For the gift of time with her."

78. The Teardrop
(Also in Nadia's Tears)

There are times when we
Ought to do more, you see?
Still there are times in this life
Filled with pain and much strife,
When the answers don't come clearly
And we wonder why we cling so dearly
To life lost and filled with so much cost
That leaves us feeling tempest tossed.
A search of the minds all around
For the answers to be found,
Led to many a question
And one conclusion:
There are times
Simply to
Cry.

79. Good Morning

It's a good morning.
Welcome, good morning.
Welcome, fine day,
One more chance to say
All you creatures great and small
Heed the morning call
Upon your heart to sing
It's a good morning.

It's a good morning,
Not one for mourning.
The past is past now.
There's no use wondering how
Your life slipped by so quickly.
So, I say to you truly
Release this year with not one tear.
Face the morning without fear.

It's a good morning.
Welcome, good morning.

80. Healer's Love

Should your ears fail to bear these words to you
Feel them with your spirit.
Let them write upon your heart.
Let them carry your soul to a place of safety.
I told you once my love is yours.
May you hear it many more.
Hard as it is to see you like this,
Please believe me when I say,
"A love like ours cannot be conquered this way."
Part of me feels, should you perish so would I,
If not in body, then in mind,
Yet I know I would go on living.
Just to carry the part of you at one with me.
If ever love had any power,
May it be enough to heal you.
I told you once my love is yours.
May you hear it many more.

81. Love Shall Find

Love shall find whom it will.
Dear father mine, need I remind?
You taught me what a man should be.
Strong, brave, kind, and truly free
To love, honor, serve, and save.
What matters his lowborn birth?

Love shall find whom it will.
Flee not, my love. Stand with me.
I hear their words and care not.
They hold no power over me.
Should they call for my crown
I would pay that price for you.

Love shall find whom it will.
Let learned men say otherwise.
From the way my heart cries
I know this love will pass
Test of time, trial of birth,
All reasons declaring it foolishness.

Love shall find whom it will.
I should know. It found me
When I wanted nothing more
Than to flee this strange new pain.
For the world I would gain,
I choose you and our love.

82. Best Way to Say Goodbye

Trying to find the best way to say goodbye,
Couldn't think of anything profound.
Maybe we'll meet again one day.
Maybe this is goodbye forever.
Either way, it's been a privilege
To know you day by day.
As you prepare to go away, I will pray
You will bless those you meet along the way.

If you learn nothing else from me,
Learn this and learn it well.
The secret to success in life is this
Find some way to serve someone else.
Then when you need some help
They'll be there, your best friend
Your spirit's guardian.
As you prepare to go away, I will pray
You will bless those you meet along the way.

Book 2: Just Like You
And Other Inspirational Christian Poems

By Julie C. Gilbert

Table of Contents:

1. Just Like You
2. Pride
3. Strangers in this Land
4. Vision, Advice, Plea
5. My Corner
6. Why Do I Cry?
7. Sweet Dreams are Made
8. Technology
9. Half-Blind
10. Evil Whispers
11. Three Things
12. Two Stories and a Challenge
13. Arms of the Lord
14. Alive in Him
15. Follow Him
16. Battle for You
17. Captive to Indifference
18. Why Do We Cry?
19. The City
20. Steady
21. Take Time
22. Always
23. Christian Life: Not Easy but Worth It
24. For the Enemy
25. Will I Ever?
26. God Most High
27. Glorious Night
28. Puzzle Piece
29. Praise
30. Beautiful Sight

31. Liquid Prayers
32. Believe
33. Higher Calling
34. Life Beyond
35. Moonlight
36. No Time Like the Present
37. Blood and Renewal
38. Grant me Wisdom
39. Trust the Lord
40. Fingerprint of God
41. Shadowed Smiles
42. Snow Softly Fall
43. The Truth Remains
44. Prepare
45. Hand in Hand
46. No Tragedy Quite Like
47. Stronger than Loss
48. Only Way to Peace
49. Hope in Loss
50. Still Praising
51. Powerful Knowledge
52. To the Hurting
53. Worry is a Luxury
54. He Meant You
55. Promise
56. On Limits
57. Make a Difference
58. Who Needs Luck?
59. Heart of Gold
60. Holy Child
61. Unshakeable
62. Yesterday's Prayer
63. Your Eyes Say

64. Sunset

65. Christianese

66. Praise Anew

67. Strangest Dream

68. Holy Spirit Fire

69. Undeserved Cross

70. Perfect Rest

71. Sense of Worth

72. Simple Battle Cry

73. Awaken

74. Rest in Me

75. Catch the Vision

76. One Family

77. Moonshine

78. Come Alive

79. Pride and Joy

80. Standing Still

81. Reflect the One

82. Guiding Light

1. Just Like You

You're my hope. You're my hero.
You know all I am and what I can be.
Take this hard heart and make it like yours.
Holy Father, I need your heart.

You're my heart. You're my hero.
Let my life reflect your love.
Give me eyes to see past walls.
Give me ears to hear heart cries.
Give me hands that heal in your name.
O Holy Father, I want to be just like you.

You're my Father. You're my hero.
May my spirit walk with you.
Train my mind to see the lost ones.
Tune my ears to hear your voice.
May my soul shine with your light.
Dear Holy Father, I want to be just like you.

You're my light. You're my hero.
You know all I am and what I will be.
Take this one soul and make it like yours.
Dear Dad, I want to be just like you.

2. Pride

Though others may not see,
I know the pride in me.
I was singing, "Praise God."
And thinking, "Am I on key?"
I was saying, "God is love!"
But doubting, "Can He truly love me?"
I was confessing, "I'm a sinner."
And thinking, "Hey, I'm not so bad."
And yet forever and ever I am blessed,
For in my God I shall find my rest.
He is faithful to forgive all of my sins
Again and again and again.

3. Strangers in this Land

Once, long ago, God came to Earth.
Once, long ago, Christ died for all.
I believe this in my heart,
And that is why I can say …

I'm but a stranger in this land.
My true home lies elsewhere.
I'll make it there one day,
But for now, there's work to do.

Do you believe that Christ died for you?
Do you believe that you can be saved?
Do you believe that God's for you?
If this is so, then you and I …

We're only strangers in this land.
Our true home lies elsewhere.
We'll make it there one day,
But for now, there's work to do.

There are others in this world.
They need to hear this truth we have.
They need to know about God's grace,
Then, they'll realize that …

They're only strangers in this land.
Their true home lies elsewhere.
They'll make it there one day,
But for now, there's work to do.

4. Vision, Advice, Plea

I had a vision late last night.
You can call me crazy,
But this is my tale:
A Christian stood at the gates of Heaven
And waited as the gatekeeper referenced a book.
Finally, the angel looked up, smiled, and said,
"You're on my list, He's paid the price…welcome
home!"

Now, I craned my neck as far as I could,
And I caught a glimpse of a gaping wound …
A Christian stood at the gates of Heaven,
And he cried his last tears …
Before walking through, he said,
"I am happy to be home,
But I wasn't ready to go home today.
I had so many plans … so many goals …
So many dreams left undreamed."
Then, he vanished into light.

Well, what does that mean?
What can I learn?
I don't have all the answers,
But here are a few random thoughts.

Every Christian should serve the Lord
In every way they possibly can.
For you never really know the future.
One day, you could suddenly find yourself
Watching the gatekeeper search for your name.

He'll find your name and welcome you home.
And you'll shed your last tears.
Before walking through, you'll say,
"I wasn't ready to go home today …"
Then, you'll vanish into light.

Well, what does that mean?
What can I learn?
Here are a few more random thoughts.

Every non-Christian ought to consider this:
There's no better time than the present time
To get things right with the Lord.
He's paid the price; the gift is free.
Won't you reach out and take it?

Now, if you're thinking, "That's nice,
But I don't believe in Heaven or Hell."
All I can say is consider this:
Whether you believe or not, they're there,
You're so much more than flesh and blood!
You have an eternal home somewhere.
Where that home is … Is totally up to you.

Well, if it's a battle, I will fight it.
With God on my side, I cannot fail.
Through all things uncertain in life
This rare truth shines as a beacon
Of hope to all God's own.

5. My Corner

Though plans fail, fade, and change
Peace reigns in my corner,
That quiet place where worry
Used to rule over
Me, now no more.

Time enough slipped by
While I cowered in my corner.
I'll make my plans
Then waste no time reliving
Each moment.

When I'm worn and slowly fading
I'll retreat to my corner
Where chaos cannot follow
There I'll stay and renew
My faith by prayer.

With Christ in me I am perfectly
At peace in my corner,
This quiet place where I worship
Him who rules over
Me, now and ever more.

6. Why Do I Cry?

I sit, surrounded by my tears
And wonder why I cry.
Do I cry for the lost of this world?
Do I cry for turmoil and pain?
Do I cry for some catastrophe?
Do I cry for my own little wants?

All of these reasons are correct,
Though they are not all right.
There is much to cry about.
There is much that gets one down.
There is no reason this time.
There is only God, and me, and tears …
Until some thoughts come to me,
And I must smile.
My God died to save the lost.
My God can cure all pain.
My God is rightly in control.
My God is always a source of strength.

7. Sweet Dreams are Made

Sweet dreams may seem to be fantasies,
But sweet dreams are made of more than these.
They soothe away fear and pain.
Sweet dreams may seem mere happy things
That momentarily divert the mind.
Can you feel it?
This world is dying slowly.
Tragedy strikes around us.
Mankind wars to rule.
People die from hate
And suffer under words flung hastily.
Disease claims some, disaster others.
Both quite natural yet so unnatural.
It wasn't meant to be this way.
Choice led to sin,
And the rest is history.
Do not become cold.
Ask God for sweet dreams.
He will take your burdens,
Setting your mind at ease.
Such is the purpose of sweet dreams.

8. Technology

We dream that technology will deliver us.
We dream of an age of wisdom.
We dream yet forget to enjoy this life.
It is possible to talk to three
Thousand people in an hour
And never learn the name of one.
It is possible to buy your heart's desire
Good or evil, from a musty basement,
Hidden away from everyone.
It is possible to spend untold hours
In a virtual world where you
Can pretend to be anyone.
So much for this age of wisdom.
So much for this new religion.
So much for technology.
I'm not saying it's a curse,
But sin twisted this gift into an irresistible idol.
Once again, we'll worship creation,
Forgetting the Creator.
Seeking freedom, power, peace
And not remembering why.
We dream that technology will deliver us.
We dream of an age of wisdom.
We dream yet forget to enjoy this life.

Just Like You

9. Half-Blind

I can see, but I can't see.
My head is playing tricks on me.
It was only two tiny drops,
But now my eyes are quite useless.
What a reminder that I am fragile!
I know it's temporary,
But this is really scary.
Can't even read the words I write.
Dare I trust myself with a car?
No, I am stuck here for a time.
Half-blind, that describes me well.
Half-blind is also a spiritual state.
Many see, but they do not see.
I pray, dear God, open their eyes!

10. Evil Whispers

What will you do?
What will you do
When the evil one comes
To whisper in your ear.
"You don't need to pray today
Didn't you pray yesterday?
What good can prayer do now?
Look at how much you have to do!
What's one more hour?
What's one more minute?
Just put if off for a while …"

If you hear these thoughts
The best thing to do is pray right away.
What will it do?
It will unburden your heart
And lift your spirits up.
Prayer will lead you to the throne,
Right to the Holy One,
To the only one who can make you smile
Through all pain.
Let Him unburden your heart.

11. Three Things

Are you a slave to apathy?
What you want to do
You can't bring yourself
To care enough to carry out.
There are three things that will set you free
From a deep sense of apathy:
Jesus, Jesus, and more Jesus.

Only God's Son ever led a perfect life.
Only God's Son ever earned the right
To be the faultless sacrifice
To heal our broken world.

Are you a slave to your sin?
What you don't want to do
You can't stop yourself
From craving every day.
There are three things that will set you free
From sin's strong claim over you:
Jesus, Jesus, and more Jesus.

12. Two Stories and a Challenge

Story One: One day, a child asked just this:
"How will the work of the Lord be done?
This world's so big, and there are so many
Lost who need to hear."

This was the answer the child received:
Some will go far to serve the Lord.
Some will go far indeed
To foreign lands to serve the Lord.

Others will stay right here at home.
Others will stay home to serve.
And so, in this way all will hear,
And all work will be done right.

Story Two: One day, an angel asked just this:
"Who will go far to serve the Lord?
Who will go far to foreign lands
To serve the Lord far from home?"

Some answered that in just this way:
"I will go far to serve the Lord.
I will go far to foreign lands
To serve the Lord where need may rise."

Then, the angel asked just this:
"Who will stay here to serve the Lord?
Who will stay right here
And serve the Lord from their home?"

Others answered in just this way:
"I will stay here to serve the Lord.
I will stay right here
And serve the Lord where need may rise."

Challenge: Now, consider where you are:
Will you answer the call of the Lord?
Whether you stay or go far away,
Serve the Lord with all your heart!"

13. Arms of the Lord

This world may seem cold and cruel.
Do not despair. There's still good here.
Everything touched by God's hand
Shines with His glory.
When trouble comes your way
Step into His loving arms.
Trust me.
You are better off in the arms of the Lord.
You are better off in the arms of the One
Who loved you so much He died
While you were still the enemy.

Now, sometimes people die for their friends,
But few and far between
And none who were perfect,
Save our Lord Christ,
Willingly sacrificed for the enemy.
His arms are always open.
Wait not for tragedy to receive comfort.
Trust me.
You are better off in the arms of the Lord.
You are better off in the arms of the One
Who loved you so much He died
While you were still the enemy.

14. Alive in Him

Welcome to life in Christ.
Sit back and hold on tight.
It'll be quite a ride.
You'll have your ups and downs,
But as you wait for pending doom,
Let the sweet scent of a rose
Carry you far away.
Now you know you're alive.
Hallelujah, praise the Lord,
You're alive in Him!

Hear the wind move through the leaves.
Feel its soft kiss touch your face
And take a deep breath.
Now you know you're alive.
Hallelujah, praise the Lord,
You're alive in Him!

Cast your gaze upon the ocean.
Can you see its end?
So shall you never see the end
Of God's love for you.
Now you know you're alive.
Hallelujah, praise the Lord,
You're alive in Him!

15. Follow Him

God doesn't need me, but He wants me,
As He want you, as He want us to follow Him.
So, let us follow Him.
To walk by faith is no easy task,
But we'll make it through.
He will give us strength,
And we will walk on.
So, let us follow Him.
One step in the right direction.
One step is all it takes
To start us on the right path.
We will live our lives to serve the Lord our God,
And He will lift us up.
So, let us follow Him.
God doesn't need us, but He wants us
To follow Him each and every day.
So, let us pray.
For to walk by faith is no easy task,
But we'll make it through.
He will give us strength,
And we will walk on.
So, let us follow Him.

Julie C. Gilbert

16. Battle for You

Do you feel them watching you,
Guiding your every step,
Telling you right from wrong
That doesn't line up with
Something deep in your soul?
I can see them whisper in your ears.
There's a battle on and it's for you.
The deceiver's lies are so lovely
His promise so sweet.
It's a web of lies meant
To drag you down.
Do not worry.
There's a battle on, and it's for you.
Christ came and won the victory.
You have only to claim new life.

17. Captive to Indifference

Do you understand the times?
Do you understand that we are
Captives to a culture of indifference?
We can see the problems,
And we feel helpless to help.
A thousand thoughts stand in the way
Not the least being:
Your problems are not my problems.
We offer meaningless words like
"Sorry for you pain
Wish I could help, but I can't.
So, have a nice day."
What does that mean to the hurting heart?
If you can't find proper words,
Just hold your tongue and listen well.
The truth may be you can't do a thing.
But you can change your heart,
Offer a prayer, release your chains,
And quit being a captive to this
Culture of indifference.

18. Why Do We Cry?

Tell me why, o why, why do we cry?
Why do we live and suffer, only to die?

Why does it rain?
And why is there pain?
Why does the wind blow so fast?
And why is my life racing past?

People are dying all around.
Nowhere is there peace to be found.

I'll tell you why, o why, why we do cry.
Why we live, suffer, and die.

Once upon a time, nothing was wrong,
Then this crafty snake came along.
The first man and woman did sin,
And it seemed as if Satan did win.
But God had mercy on the lost human race.
So, He sent his Son to die in our place.

So why, o why, do we still cry?
Why do we suffer and die?
I can tell you why.

The cause of all our pains
Is that evil still reigns.
This is why we cry.
This is why we suffer and die.

I tell you do not despair

Just Like You

Over the fact that life's not fair.
One day things will be set right.
We'll join hands in Heaven, much to our delight.

Come, join us, one and all
Let God change you from "Saul" to "Paul."
Accept the free gift,
And your burdens God will lift.

19. The City

You and I, we're on a journey
Walking to a city far away,
Beautiful, bright, and clean always.
Pure gold lines the streets.
Joy's common as dust here.
Night and day mean nothing there.
Hearts are light and fixed upon
The Holy One who fills the air.
Let us praise Sovereign God!

Sounds nice.
There's just one thing:
A high wall surrounds that place,
And there's only one gate.
No siege can succeed.
No man can storm that gate
Nor buy entrance with money
Or earn his way by good deeds.
Never fear, there's a way:
Jesus Christ mans that gate.
You're paid in full, walk on through.
The gate lies open to all who
With childlike hearts believe.

20. Steady

What responsibilities do you and I have
To this place we call home?
The world is warming.
The water is rising.
Our fate could be seen as
Steady as the wind.

Steady as the wind.
Steady as good fortune.
Steady as the moonlight
Shining on the ocean.

By and by there comes a time
With naught to do but cry.
That time may be not too far away,
But for now, there's still time
To change this fate.
What can you and I do
To make our world
Steadier than the wind?

21. Take Time

I know you are busy.
I know you are worried,
But I want you to know you should
Take time to worship,
Take time to pray,
"Lord, please help me through life today."
Take the time just to say,
"God, I love You."

Nothing else could ease your mind
Quite like the peace of God
Flowing through and bidding you
Take time to worship,
Take time to pray,
"God, bless the works of my mind today."
Take the time just to say,
"God, I love You."

Not much in life is a guarantee,
But rest assured, if you trust the Lord,
You're in good hands.
So, take time to worship,
Take time to pray,
"Thank You, Father, for my life today."
Take the time just to say,
"God, I love You."

22. Always

You are always. You are for all days.
Not only Sundays. Not only Mondays.
Not only some days.
You are for always.

Fill our minds. Tune our hearts.
Heal everything wrong
In our heads, in our hearts,
Deep down in our spirits.
O Lord, make us come alive.

You are always. You are for all days.
Not only Wednesdays and Fridays.
Not only Saturdays.
Not only Tuesday, Thursday prayers.
Not only some days. You are for always.
You are always.

O God, give us new life.
Give us fresh hearts and deep love
For this lost and broken world.
Carry our spirits beyond the here and now.
There's a war we cannot see,
And we need your weapons to be free.

You are always. You are for all days.
Not only for weekends and free time.
Not only here and now.
You are for always.
You are always.

23. Christian Life: Not Easy but Worth It

So, you say somebody told you
That the life of a Christian would be easy.
I can tell you right now, they lied.
Maybe they didn't mean it.
Maybe they had a better motive in mind.
But all the same, I still maintain, they lied.

We're prone to anger, fear, and pain.
The only difference is that we have hope
Of a better time and a better place.
For one day God will return,
Then anger, fear, and pain will fade away
Like morning mist when the burning
sun decides to show its face.

Though the life of a Christian won't be easy,
It certainly won't leave you worse off
Then you are right now.
The hope and the peace that come from
Loving God and letting Him love you
Will more than make you ready to face the world.

24. For the Enemy

Today, I pray for the enemy.
For all those who hate my country.
For all those willing to take lives.
For all those who do not believe.
May they come to a saving
Knowledge of the Holy One.
What better testimony could there be
Than to turn somebody who would
Kill for a cause
Into somebody who would die
For the sake of the cross?

These people do not lack fervor,
But their hearts are cold as ice
And they lie in the clutches of the evil one.
He will drag countless to Hell.
It's a very sad thing to see.
I cannot change too much,
But today I pray for the enemy:
"Lord, work Your will in them."

25. Will I Ever …

Will I ever learn to be
Patient at all times?
Sometimes I ask myself,
"Why's life got to be so dang complicated?"

See, I started out singing
Lovely praises to my King,
But it turned into a complaining fest
Where I spent time crying out,
"O God, why shut these doors?
Where do You want me to be?
Where am I headed?
I want so bad to be Yours and Yours alone,
But my heart's prone to pride
And my mind wanders
Far away from Your side."

Father, come and teach me
How to praise You properly.
You are Holy and just
And good all the time.

Will I ever be able to say
All I am and ever shall be
Is ever only truly Yours?

26. God Most High

Wish I knew a thousand languages.
Wish I could speak with my hands.
Wish I could say what's on my heart
Some better way.

Even if I had a thousand days.
Even if I tried a hundred ways.
I'd just begin to describe
God most high!

There are no words
Good enough to describe His majesty.
There are no words
Great enough to encompass His glory.

The highest mountains and the open seas
May dazzle and mystify
These are dim in beauty
When compared to God most high!

He possesses wisdom, power, perfect love.
He is timeless, ageless, matchless.
Nothing can compare or compete
With God most high!

27. Glorious Night

Have you truly experience glorious night?
Hear my tale then decide.

On a cool summer's eve,
I shut my eyes tightly,
Thinking just maybe if I listened hard
I would find glorious night.

Exploring the world with only sound,
I could not help but be amazed
By the sweet sounds that soothed my soul.
I listened to the tiny ones
Sing soft praises and wondered
When I last sang my heart out just like that.

My eyes flew open
And fell upon that lesser light.
Like any good ruler it sometimes
Shines less to let us feast our eyes
Upon the starry hosts.

I cannot help but be amazed
By the matchless beauty seen anew
Each and every glorious night!

28. Puzzle Piece

I am only one tiny piece
In this giant puzzle,
And I don't know where I go,
But I can trust in this:
There is a master plan.
There is a holy plan.
There is a place for me in this world,
And God will show me
Where to go when its time.

Waiting has never been a strong
Point that I could claim.
So, I'll follow my heart,
Trusting in this fact:
There is a master plan.
There is a holy plan.
There is a place for me in this world,
And God will show me
How to act when its time.

I shall never have to truly
Worry for a lack of direction,
For I know this one fact.
I can always trust that:
There is a master plan.
There is a holy plan.
There is a place for me in this world,
And God will show me
What to do when its time.

29. Praise

I want to shout to all the world
That God is Lord over all.
I want to praise His Holy name
With every breath that I take.
For if I could praise the Lord God
With every breath that I take,
Well, then, I would be
The happiest person in all of this Earth.
For the chief end of man
Is to praise the Lord with all of our hearts.

God loves all of us.
He's offered us peace through His own Son.
So, I will praise his holy name.
From dawn 'til dusk and far beyond,
I want to shout for all to hear
That God is Lord over all.
So, won't you join in?
And together we will, for all of time
Praise the Lord our God.

30. Beautiful Sight

It's hard to imagine
The love God has for us.
For when we fear, fail, or fall,
He hears us as we call,
Then wraps us in a peace so perfect
We can only bow our hearts,
Open our mind's eye, and boldly declare,

"You're a beautiful sight.
You make all things all right.
Though this world wants to fall
All to pieces everywhere.
You're a beautiful sight.
You make all things all right.
You're a beautiful sight
To this weary soul."

Come free my heart from angry
Shadows of the past.
They hold me here
To doubt, sin, and shame.
I am ready to move on!
For I know that you are …
You're a beautiful sight!
You make all things all right!
You're a beautiful sight
To this weary soul.

31. Liquid Prayers
(Also included in *Beyond Broken Pencils*)

One week slipped by, then almost two.
Each moment made the pain recede,
But I wanted to cry.
I wanted to cry for the angry man
Who stole so many lives.
I wanted to cry for the people
Who would never see home again.
Wanted to cry for the strangers
Mourning a loved one lost.
Wanted to pour out liquid prayers
For everyone wounded in body, spirit, and soul.

Imagine my dismay when I discovered
Something deep within holds my tears at bay.
Have I seen too much to cry?
Or is there too much to cry for?

Though no tears may come,
My heart will weep.
I will weep for the angry man,
For those who fell that day,
For everyone beyond our help.
I will weep for the strangers
Whose pain may not recede.
I will pour out liquid prayers
To bind wounds of body, spirit, and soul.

32. Believe

I believe …
Good things come to those
Who call upon the Lord.

I believe …
Prayer can set wrongs to right,
Melt hearts of stone,
Bring healing and bind up brokenness.

Do not fear …
What the future holds.
For nothing can keep you captive long
If you believe.

I believe …
When darkness, hardship, and heartache
Try to sink your spirits low,
Turn to the Holy One.
Find love, hope, and peace
These are true treasures.

I believe …
Dreams come true
For those who dream big.

33. Higher Calling

There is no higher calling
Than to praise the Lord God.
There is no higher calling
Than to share this good news:
That Jesus came, lived perfectly,
Suffered, died, and conquered death
So all could be free.

There is no higher calling
But to share this news with all
Who have ears to hear, eyes to see,
Or simply an open heart to believe.

There is no higher calling
Than to cast your cares on God.
There is no higher calling
Than to help someone in need.

Now, you may ask why
All these callings are so high.
It is my estimation that every calling
To serve the Lord, whether by prayer or deed,
Is the highest calling we could receive,
So, let us serve.

34. Life Beyond

Do you ever think about
Life beyond the here and now?
Where will you be?
What will you see?
How will you handle
The problems that come your way?

I will trust the Lord to carry me through
Every trial, hardship, and pain.
If there ever was someone qualified
To hear my tale of woe and let me cry,
It would be the Lord who came to Earth to die.
He lived perfectly yet suffered greatly
All to save the lost like you and me.
Praise the Lord always.

Praise the Lord every day
Under grace we can always say,
"God is here with us!"
Because His promises are always sure,
We can live by faith, prayer, and hope
Knowing the future's in good hands.
Praise the Lord always.

35. Moonlight

I had no second chance.
I was captured with one glance.
Have you seen the moon tonight?
It is a strange and beautiful sight.
Weary drivers beware.
The moon compels one to stare.
Do not look too long
Lest you make a turn all wrong!

It's kind of hard to classify,
But I'm sure going to try.
Wonder how God made that color.
It had to be God and no other.
There is power in that light.
I could look forever and never cease
To be amazed by the beauty.

I could stare all night
With awe and delight.
Would to God all could see
Christ's love as clearly as
I see things by the moonlight!

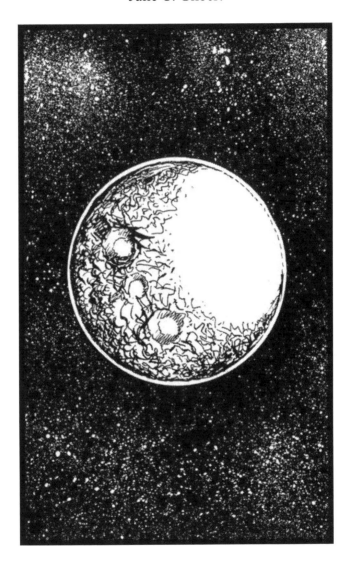

36. No Time Like the Present

There's no time like the present time
To get to know the Lord better.
What keeps my heart away?
Nothing less than a
Thousand little things of life.
And can I change all that?
Of course, I can, I just need to run to Him.

There's no time like the present time
To get to know the Lord better.
How do you keep your best friends?
Why, simply by spending time with them.
God has shown an interest in you.
Why don't you let Him
Love you as only He can?

37. Blood and Renewal

There is blood on my hands.
I know only one way to free them.

God, my God, open my heart,
Take out pride, take out pain.
Leave only mercy, love, and joy.

There is no room for regrets
For peace of mind must be prized
As the highest of riches
One can attain.

Heart, dear heart, feel no fear.
Step forth into dawn.
It is a new day.

There is blood on my hands.
I know only one way to free them.

God, my God, come work in me.
Remove all doubt, sin, and shortcomings.
Leave only You.

38. Grant Me Wisdom

God, grant me wisdom.
God, grant me peace of mind.
It's fair to say I've lost direction
If I ever knew at all.
I wish I had a more eloquent way
To speak my mind and seek Your face.
Yet this simple cry says it all.
God, grant me wisdom.
God, grant me peace of mind.
Uncertainty wants to drown me in self-pity,
But that won't give me answers.
O, I know I'll know at the right time,
Which steps to take and where to go,
Just wish You'd tell me sooner.
I like to think I trust you,
But even as I say aloud:
God, grant me wisdom.
God, grant me peace of mind.
Part of my heart is whispering
May my will be done.
I'll surrender the whispers
For the weight it holds over me
Ought not to be.
I am free in You.

39. Trust the Lord

Where will I be in ten years
And what will I be doing?
Maybe that's too far away.

Where will I be in five years
And what will I be doing?
Maybe that's too far away.

So many choices must be made.
They weigh heavily on me.

I will trust the Lord God
To lead me on the right way.
I will trust the Lord God,
For only He will never fail.

Friends and family and mentors
Of all kinds will fail at times.
Not so with the Lord my God.

On the one hand, I wish
Making decisions was much easier,
But on the other hand,
I'm glad it's hard for me.
It forces me to trust the Lord.

I will trust the Lord God
To lead me on the right way.
I will trust the Lord God,
For only He will never fail.

40. Fingerprint of God

The fingerprint of God
Can be found all around.
In the pattern of a leaf
And the cry of a baby.
In the complexity of a cell
And in the roar of thunder,
There it will be found.

The fingerprint of God
Can be found all around.
In the blaze of the sun
And in the whisper of the ocean.
In the fire of lightning
And the song of the wind,
There it will be found.

The fingerprint of God
Can be found all around.
In the smile of a child
And in the fury of a tornado.
In the dawn of a new day
And the silent slipping away of the old,
There it will be found.

41. Shadowed Smiles

There was a shadow
Over your smile today.
I'm sorry I did not see
It in time to say
I'm sorry to see
There's a shadow
Over your smile today.

I do not know all that goes
On inside your mind,
But you and I both
Know the only One
Who can take your burden,
Make it lighter, and banish
The shadows from your smile.

They may not be able to see
Your point of view.
So, we will pray that one day
The One we know
Will work all this out for good
So we can all see you smile
Without shadows once more.

42. Snow Softly Fall

See the snow softly fall.
Only God could have imagined
Such a peaceful scene.
Almost fear to take a step.
Like it's akin to throwing stones
Through stained glass.

I guess my walk here is all right.
The way the snow falls tonight
This path won't remember me anyway.
I'll turn around, wait a minute,
Watch my footsteps disappear,
Feeling the bitter chill in the air
That reminds me I am so frail.

God come warm me with Your presence.
As I pray and watch the snow softly fall,
I'm reminded of the peace and the
Steep price paid to gain my soul.
Wish the snow would softly fall every day.
Then, I'd always remember my God
Who keeps me warm with His presence.

Julie C. Gilbert

43. The Truth Remains

I read somewhere today that a
Rich man's money will ransom his life,
But a poor man hears no threats.
Is anyone better off than somebody else?
No way. The struggles may differ,
But they're there all the same.
Life's hard and quite unpredictable.
The flame of life can vanish in a flash
Or flicker uncertainly for years to come.

Eventually, everybody stands
Before the same grand throne,
Answering to the same great God.
Hearing, "Well done, O faithful one."
Or "depart from me, I know you not."
Imagine the sounds resounding around that throne!
Shouts of joy mixed with much despair.
People crying 'cause Christ died,
And they didn't care.

This picture may be a bit fanciful but
The truth remains:
Your debt is paid,
But the gift's unclaimed.
This choice concerning Jesus Christ
Will shape today, tomorrow, and forever.

44. Prepare

Do you understand the importance of preparing?
You cannot control the things that befall you,
But you can control the way you react to them.
And the key to all this is to lean
on the Lord when times are good.
So that when hard times come,
Leaning on the Lord will be
As natural as breathing,
As natural as seeing,
As natural as hoping to better your life.

45. Hand in Hand

Prayer and praise go hand in hand.
There may be some days
You just don't feel like praising at all.
You can be sure dark days will come.
Days dictated by storms of life.
Days when tears outweigh the smiles.
On such days you need to praise
Stronger, harder, longer.
The more you praise
The higher your heart will soar.

When you heart is weighed down
Prayer can be the cure.
Prayer and praise go hand in hand.
It doesn't matter how well you sing,
So long as it's straight from you soul.
Whether you praise by raising hands,
Bowing your head, or simply closing eyes,
You can be sure God hears.
Always remember prayer and praise
Go so well hand in hand.

46. No Tragedy Quite Like

I read of pain in a far-off place.
Wondered why God let this tragedy strike.
This storm may not touch my shore,
But it sure rocked their shores.
Well, what can I do?
I don't know but I know
There's no tragedy quite like apathy
In the face of tragedy.
Will a prayer really make a difference?
Will money really solve the problems?
In despair, we seek somebody to blame,
Though it's nobody's fault.
Blame can't change this tragedy,
But there's still hope in the Lord.
He can bring you through the pain.
Maybe I can't do much for you,
But you have my prayers every day.
There's no tragedy quite like apathy
In the face of tragedy.
There's no hope quite like hope found in Christ.
It's this hope I wish on you.

47. Stronger than Loss

I cannot say I understand
Exactly what you're feeling.
I feel stunned though I'm on
The edge of this tragedy.

The only mother I ever lost
I never knew,
But I can well imagine the aching loss,
Thinking of how I'd feel in your place.

I can't do much but cling to the cross,
Believing with my heart
What my head already knows:
My God is stronger than loss.

My God pours peace enough to fill the oceans.
When my strength's gone like it so oft is,
I'll hold onto His peace-filled promises,
Knowing my God is stronger than loss.

Let the pain wash through you.
I'll be here to share it.
We can rest in the promise:
Our God is stronger than loss.

48. Only Way to Peace

So, it seems like your whole world
May fall apart around you.
What will you do?
Where will you turn?
Who will you trust in
To carry you through
All of these hard times?

Some may trust in their own selves
To make it through,
And that may work for a time,
But in the end, only those who
Trust in God will be left standing.
Christ is ready. He is willing.
He will hold your hand
And walk you through
Each and every trial.

So, when trouble comes your way
There's not much to say
Except the only way to peace
Is through Jesus Christ's blood.

49. Hope in Loss

Heard you lost your best friend,
And your heart's still hurting.
Heard you're having a tough time
Moving on with life.
I won't claim to know
The depths of such pain,
But I wanted you to hear
Many times in many ways:
You are loved.

There is power in prayer.
There is hope in loss.

Call upon the Great Comforter.
Let Him heal the wounds in your soul.

Love so deep you can feel
Its absence as a void
Can be reclaimed
In sweet memories.
Hold them dear in heart and mind.
Know you are loved.

There is power in prayer.
There is hope in loss.

Peace of mind's not always easy to find,
But it comes from above
And in knowing you are loved.

50. Still Praising

This pain in my mouth in my head
May drive me to silence,
But if I fall silent,
Know that inside I'm still singing.
I'm still praising. I'm still saying,
"You are the best thing in my life!"

This pain in my mouth in my head
May drive me to tears,
But if I start crying,
Know that inside I'm still praising,
For You know all of my pain.
And one day, I'll look back
And remember You were here!

One more day and one more night.
One more moment to reflect.
I'll sing aloud or in my head.
You are God and You are good!
I'll cry out "Praise Your name!"
So the rocks may keep their silence.

51. Powerful Knowledge

My prayers are with you.
I didn't know you had so many problems.
I've been consumed with my own.
Forgive me for the lapse in
Seeing you are hurting.
When you feel weak
Just close your eyes,
Shut out demanding world,
Tune your ear to God,
And let His peace pour over you.

My prayers are with you.
When you're weak then you're strong,
For then you know for sure
You can't make it on you own.
This knowledge is pure power.
Lay still and let tears fall.
They will wash your burdens
And make them ready to be laid bare
To the Holy One, to the only one
Who lift them off your soul.

52. To the Hurting

To the hurting,
I do not know the extent of your pain.
As far as life goes,
You've seen more pain than I have,
And I don't envy you that.
You've seen more anger, more strife,
More heartache than I have,
But I'm asking you to remember this:
There are times when
Humans are a pretty poor representation
Of our Heavenly Father.
Please remember that there are times when
Humans are a pretty poor representation
Of the love and grace shown at the cross
For this lost human race.
Always remember through all of your pain
That God is the perfect one.

To the hurting,
I do not know the extent of your pain,
But I do know that God is a comforter.
Cast yourself in His arms and in the end
You will find the strength to go on …
Even through pain.

53. Worry is a Luxury

When trouble threatens to overthrow your mind,
Remember Job's words.
He'd just found out
Wealth and children and most things
Precious to him were gone,
Yet he had the courage to say:
"The Lord gave, and the Lord has taken away
May the name of the Lord be praised."
Wish I could say the same
If such a lot fell to me,
But I will not worry.
Worry is luxury we cannot
Endure for long with a sound mind.
It tears at sanity one thread at a time.
There is far too much trouble
To go borrowing more.
Take comfort, God knows your breaking point.
Fortify you heart with the Word
Then worry can never conquer you.

54. He Meant You

Yesterday started strangely.
I met Jesus in a dream.
At first, I couldn't understand,
Then, I learned to listen deep inside.

He told me more than could fill one dream.
The pieces I remember
Make me want to know more.

He said life was more than it seemed.
I shouldn't let it slip on by.
Sometimes a good cry and a deep sigh
Are needed to reclaim a sense of calm.

As he turned to walk away,
I called out, "Jesus! Where are you going?"
He said, "I am going to meet a friend.
She is coming home today."

Somehow, I just knew
When he said those words,
He meant you.

The realization released a strange tide:
Joy and sorrow and pain
With a shred of peace at knowing
Our loss was Heaven's gain.

55. Promise

I want to know …
I want to see …
I want to praise …
The God of this universe.

For He is Holy
And He is mighty
And He is perfect
In every way imaginable.

And the best part of all
Is that He loves me
And he died for me
To set me free from all of my sin.

So, now I am His
And for all of time
I will serve
This my God, my Lord, and King.

56. On Limits

There is nothing
Too big or too small
For my God.

He has hung each star out in the sky.
He has seen into the hearts of man.
He has watched over sparrows.
He has clothed fields in flowers.

There is nothing
On Earth or in Heaven or in places unseen
That can't be reached
By my God.

There is nothing
Too big or too small
For my God.

57. Make a Difference

All who are Christian have a hope
Half the world dreams of
And most never find.
Listen carefully to the instructions
Given by God in infinite wisdom.
Then, apply His principles to your life.
So simple to say, yet hard to do!
But God as my witness,
You'll make a difference
If you apply yourself heart, soul, and mind.
Seek out higher things,
Strive for perfection,
Yet fear not to fail.
Love your neighbor,
Care for your brother,
Encourage your sister,
And above all seek God.
He will shine through you
Then, God as my witness,
You'll make a difference!

58. Who Needs Luck?

I want to know the truth.
Sure it might be dangerous,
But I've got to know the truth.
You can wish me luck
Along this perilous path.
But who needs luck when you've got
God on your side?

I want to know the truth.
Whether I live or die lies in God's hands.
So, worry not for me.
If the enemy succeeds in
Separating body and soul
I'll be on my way home.

I want to know the truth.
Truth is worth sacrifice.
With a little bit of luck
The danger will pass swiftly.
But who needs luck
When you've got God on your side?

59. Heart of Gold

Some are gifted in the arts.
Some are gifted with hearts of gold.
I know somebody like this.
Most people care for their friends,
But it takes a heart of gold to care
For the downtrodden stranger.
Where'd this heart of gold come from?
I believe everyone has a heart of gold
Buried beneath much selfishness.
Imagine the difference if a few more people
Dug deep down inside, found their
Heart of gold, and acted in love.
It wouldn't be a perfect world,
But some change is better than
No change at all.
Change can be realized by a
Few more people with hearts of gold.

60. Holy Child

What do you think of when
You think of Christmas?
Is it candy; is it gifts?
Is it time spent with your family?
What do you think of when
You think of Christmas?
Is all the stress you get
When thinking of the things to be done?

No matter which side you're on …
There's something neat, there's something sweet
About the notion of our Father God
Coming down to Earth as a little child,
Fully God and fully man,
Tempted in every way, yet always triumphing!

There's something neat, there's something sweet
About the notion of our Holy God
Coming down to Earth as a little child,
Destined to live perfectly,
Destined to be our sacrifice,
Praise God for this Holy child!

No matter what consumes your mind,
Take a moment to reflect upon the
Essence of Christmas:
God's only Son; the greatest gift.
Thank God for this Holy child!

61. Unshakeable

I am not worried,
Merely anxious to know the truth
About a future that lies out of my hands.
There will a time of great joy
When the heart is light
And the eyes dance merrily.
Those days, bright days, will come.
Praise God, they will come.

There will be a time for many tears
When doubt and fear rule the day.
Those days, dark days, will come.
One truth I cling to:
God is unshakeable.

He is Love and He loves me.
I made Him my cornerstone
So sickness, pain, fear, and dread
May turn my world upon its head,
Yet no dark power can steal
The peace in my heart.
It is unshakeable
'Cause it is from God.
I am unshakeable
When I lean on God.

62. Yesterday's Prayer

Did you know that I prayed
For you yesterday?
Well, neither did I, but I prayed that
God would bring comfort to all those
Who are hiding the hurt.
Draw strength from the Lord, my friend,
For no dark time can withstand
The light of His love.

Did you know that I prayed for you yesterday?
Well, neither did I, but I prayed that
God would grant wisdom to all those
Who seek His face.
I know not the hour or the day
A still small voice did declare
"Yesterday's prayers are answered today."

63. Your Eyes Say

Life concerns control your spirit.
I can read as much in your eyes.
They say, "I don't know where I'm going
And that concerns me to the core."
I'd say do not worry if I
Thought it would do any good.
But I can read the rebuttal in your eyes.
They say, "You don't know all my problems.
It's too easy to say don't worry
When you're not in my shoes."

All that is true, far too true.
Maybe the time is just not right
For you to unburden your soul to me,
But I have one suggestion that may
Help you reclaim a sense of peace.
Push all thoughts but the Lord
From your mind for a moment.
You will find Him if you seek Him,
And you will have peace when you find Him.
This holds true forevermore.

64. Sunset

Have you ever stopped
Just to watch the sunset?
It's a beautiful sight!
"Beautiful" only begins to describe
The magnitude of beauty held
In each fading ray as the sun
Seems to say, "Goodbye, until the new day …"
Some may think that sunrise
Out beautifies sunset any day.
I will take their word for that
Because I'm too lazy
To get up that early and check.
Besides, if sunrise is anything
Like its counterpart,
"Breathtakingly beautiful" will only begin to
Describe the glorious dawn of a new day.
Every night God paints the sky
Using every color imaginable.
Truly every sunset is different,
And quite a sight indeed.
If you ever forget "beautiful"
Go watch the sunset.

65. Christianese

Anyone ever think that we
Make no sense sometimes?
We say things like
"Bring it to the cross."
And "lay your burdens down."
When all we mean is
"Take your cares to God."

Anyone ever think that we
Make no sense sometimes?
We say things like
"We live in a dark, fallen world,"
And "we are lost without the Lord."
When we mean
"Sin's everywhere, and God saves."

Anyone ever think that we
Make no sense sometimes?
We say things like
"Jesus is the Lamb of God,"
And "Hallelujah, I'm set free!"
Meaning:
"God sent His Son to die for me, and I am happy!"

Why is it easy for Christians
To get stuck on Christianese?
That I could not tell you.
All I can say is that when you do be sure
To give your victim a clue.
For no one likes to be
Stuck lost in Christianese.

66. Praise Anew

I wish I knew some way
To praise You anew each day.
For as each day slips on by
I find myself wondering why
I let myself get all wrapped up
In things that fill my cup,
Yet leave me so empty
When You're the Lord of plenty.

I wish I knew some way
To praise You anew each day.
So, come now, Lord and Father,
Move the rock that is my heart farther
Down along the paths where you hide
Secret treasures for those who can abide.
Give us patience, give us strength.
Give us passion enough to go the length.

I wish I knew some way
To praise You anew each day.
Come, place a song in me,
Then in a short while set it free
To rise and fall.
Teach my heart to heed Your call
To pray and praise with every breath,
Lest I forget the One who gives me rest.

67. Strangest Dream

Awakening from the strangest dream,
I wondered what it could all mean.
I determined to write it down
Until the meaning could be found.
Something told me it would be profound
For its sheer simplicity.

I found myself in a place
Much like this, yet with some trace
Of a dark taint to the morning air.
Imagine my surprise
That upon sunrise
Shadows sprang forth everywhere.

These were no ordinary shadows.
They possessed a nature as cold as gallows
The morning after the doomed has died.
They surrounded strangers
Who knew not the dangers
And assailed their hearts and minds.

As I felt my strength slowly slip away
I knew I needed help without delay.
Words would not come to cry for aid,
Yet answers welled up in my soul:
Only the Lord can keep you whole
In a place where spirits strive.

68. Holy Spirit Fire

Holy Spirit Fire, light us up from inside.
Illuminate the future in our thoughts,
In our hopes, and in our dreams.
Show us all we need to know
To proclaim your truths across the land.
Holy Spirit Fire, light us up from inside.
In the highest halls of power
and in the deepest, darkest pits,
There's a war on for the hearts and souls of men.
Holy Spirit Fire, light us up from inside.
Knit our hearts into one.
We need your heart to understand
The love you hold for every kind of man.
Teach us more of your ways.
Whisper the deep truths into our souls.
Bring us back to life.
Holy Spirit Fire, light us up from inside.
Do not let us trade your glory
For the treasures of this Earth.
Heaven awaits our homecoming
But there is much work to finish here.
Holy Spirit Fire, light us up from inside.

Julie C. Gilbert

69. Undeserved Cross

It is my hope and fervent prayer
That as you listen to my tale
Some might come to know my Lord.
He's my hope and one true sword.
With Him dwelling deep within
No power can bind me to my sin.

Once upon a time
I led a life sublime
Large family and things aplenty
Still it seemed mighty empty.
Just as I started to despair
I was told of Christ hanging up there
On a cross he did not deserve,
The lives of all to preserve.

At first, I could not comprehend.
What kind of madness would send
An innocent to stand in our stead?
The message was far beyond my head.
Then one day I just knew
What they said had to be true.
The Kingdom belongs to true believers
The truest believers are receivers
Of His freely offered grace,
The one ticket to that place.

Some may say I've had it kind of hard.
I know I am blessed by far.
Just as I started to despair
I remembered Christ hanging up there

174

Just Like You

On a cross he did not deserve
The lives of all to preserve,
Whether they would call on Him
Or remain content in all their sin.
May it never be said
He stood in vain in your stead.

70. Perfect Rest

There's no magic in words I say.
No power on my own,
But I know the One who holds
The heavens in His hands.
We may never know the reason
Why pain reigns upon the Earth.
Still, we trust in Him.

Father God, Holy Prince,
Take our brokenness.
Take our failures.
Renew our spirits.
Remake our bodies.
Bind our wounds and soothe our souls.
Make us more like You each day.

Grant us courage to call down miracles.
You have brought us out of darkness
To spread hope across this land,
To release your peace everywhere.
Give us patience to face fears and foes.
Let us witness your glory.
May we find perfect rest in You.

71. Sense of Worth

My life like my breath like my mind.
They are gifts from God above
Whose love is matchless.
The more I study how this body works,
The more amazement drives words from my lips.
So is born a sense of worth
Guarded deep in my heart.

I didn't know there were
So many kinds of pain.
Physical, mental, emotional, just to name a few.
The infamous they may say
I don't fit the formula for
Beauty, height, or grace but
Nobody can steal my sense of worth.

Whether you believe or not
God made each person wonderfully unique.
Part of the adventure that is life
Is discovering your gifts.
They can say all they want but
Nobody can steal sense of worth.
It's innate; it's in me and
I'm in God, come what may,
My heart and mind are always safe.

72. Simple Battle Cry

An awakening awaits around the corner.
Can you feel your soul stirring?
There's a darkness creeping in,
But the Light within won't be denied.

When the trials of this world
Try to sink your soul down,
Let your heart sing out:
"Hallelujah! Hallelujah! Hallelujah!"

It's a simple battle cry.
No use wondering why.
Cling to this truth and walk on:
Love will triumph over evil.

Don't you know God wins?
The story finishes in a different age.
But until that day
When the Lord makes all things right,
You can always rest in Him.
Sing: "Hallelujah! Hallelujah!"
Let His peace invade your heart
And your soul will find rest.

73. Awaken

It's been a long time coming,
But at last I see past
The many lies you're telling me.

Why tell me lies with your eyes?
Why tell me you don't care?
Why say it doesn't matter,
When very clearly your heart's
Crying out?

You were meant for
so much more than this.
You were meant for so much more.

Come alive, dear child.
Come alive inside.
Awaken your heart and mind.
You were meant for so much more.

74. Rest in Me

Will you hear my voice
When I call your name?
Will you hear my voice
When I call you?

Will you go, my child?
Will you go?
Will you go where
I send you?

Find peace in this one truth:
No power of man,
No scheme of Hell,
Can take you from my arms.

You are blameless, pure, and holy
When you rest in me.
O, let my love purify.
Let my love renew you.

Your debt, my deed,
It's all done.
Come home and rest in me.

75. Catch the Vision

There's no doubt life's rough
But all those who trust in Christ
Will find true peace.
Once we find peace, let us share.
This is our vision: we will
Love the world, make friends, and pray.
Will you catch this vision? (2X)

Christianity is not hit and run war
It's a revolution.
It may take over your life,
But it sure is worth it!
Would you die for Christ?
Most brave souls would say yes,
But will you catch this vision? (2X)

Will you catch this vision to
Share Christ's love with
All those He died for?
There's a price to pay
And it might be steep at times.
Are you willing to sacrifice to save a life?
Will you catch this vision? (2X)

76. One Family

You may not know who I am,
But if you know the Lord
Then you know who I serve.
And if this is true then you and I
We belong to one family.

We are united in God,
United in Christ, united through the Spirit,
For the three are one.
And since this is true, you and I,
We belong to one family.

You may not know who I am
But one day you will if we both know the Lord.
For the blood of Christ covers us all,
And we will meet one day in Heaven.
And this is true because you and I
We belong to one family.

Now as one family let us serve
All the hopeless that are in this world.
We will serve through our lives;
We will serve through our works,
But most of all let us show them
The love that Christ showed us.
Now that we can hope, we must share
And bring the lost into our family.

77. Moonshine

Last night
We shared something special.
I know you wish you'd shared
That moment with your boyfriend, not best
Friend, and that's all right.
You asked me for my thoughts,
And I could not answer.
I was thinking about the moonshine
Streaming off of your eyes,
And just how crazy he must be
To not see what I see.
If that boy doesn't learn
How to treat a woman
One day, he's going to hurt for it.
If only he'd have been here
Last night.
He'd have seen the moonshine
Coming off of your eyes,
And he'd have never left
Your side.

78. Come Alive

The world says: Worry about today.
Worry about tomorrow.
Store up treasures of the Earth.
Live for the moment.
Fight for yourself
'Cause nobody cares for you like you.

I say: There may be some truths in there,
But they're all wrapped up in lies.
Treasures of Earth fade with time.
Live in the moment,
But fight for your future.
'Cause nobody cares for you like God.

Can you hear His voice?

He says: "Dear child,
I am yours and you are mine.
There's no way to earn my favor.
You have had it since time began.
It's a free gift,
But it still needs to be received.
Let my love transform your life."

Then you will be able to say:
"There is joy, simple joy,
Welling up inside my soul.
There is peace, perfect peace,
Reigning here inside my heart.
There is life, true life.
Flowing freely in me."

Don't you think it's well past time
For you to come alive?

79. Pride and Joy

It's been a long night, a longer day,
And this pain just won't fade away.
Still, I hear my Holy Father speaking to my soul.
He's shouting loud and clear:
"You're my baby.
I love you so much!
You're my pride and joy.
Don't you know my love is infinite?
You'll never have to earn my favor.
I don't love you for what you can do for me.
I don't love you because you love me.
I love for who you are
And who I made you to be.
I made you perfect.
I made you to embody peace.
I made you to reflect my love so clearly
That nobody can deny me.
You're my baby.
You're my pride and joy.
I'm gonna change this whole world
Through the way you carry my Son in your heart.
Just be my baby.
Be my pride and joy.
Rest in my promise that one day
Everything will be all right.
You're my baby.
You're my pride and joy."

80. Standing Still

I am guilty of standing still.
I am guilty of apathy.
I am guilty of perpetuating the idea
That the holy huddle works.

Lord, move me to take a step.
Move me to take two,
For each step I take
Leads to more, and soon,
I'll be running hard for You.

I am guilty of standing still.
I am guilty of pride of heart.
But God is God and Lord of all
And He has the power
To make great things of me.

Lord, please change me from within.
Far too often, I'm standing still
When I should be seizing the day,
And serving God with all my heart.

81. Reflect the One

See the flowers in the fields?
They are marvelous.
Hear the birds singing sweetly?
They are marvelous too.

See the stars twinkling high above?
They are beautiful.
See the moon light up the night?
That is beautiful too.

Watch the sun dance on water?
That is wonderful.
Look at me. Can't you see?
I am wonderful too.

Everything created
Reflects the one and only God.
He was and is and will
Always reign on high.

82. Guiding Light

Father God, Holy One,
Be my guiding light.
Show me what's right.
I know you hear every plea.

Please reveal the hopes and fears
That lie behind tears
Bottled up deep inside
Of those who won't show pain.

I know you see them perfectly.
So be my guiding light.
Show me what's right.
I want to know who burdens you.

Sometimes it seems peace
May be only for dreams.
Wars, fires, and randomness
End life every night.

O Lord, be our guiding light.
Show us what's right.
We know you love perfectly,
So help us cling to you.

Book 3: My Champion
And Other Inspirational Christian Poems

By Julie C. Gilbert

Table of Contents:

1. My Champion
2. On the Road of Life
3. Who Will You Call?
4. Unfair Tale
5. Fair
6. To the Captive
7. Chains are Gone
8. More Alive
9. Place for Peace
10. Jesus, Father, God
11. Prayer Tonight
12. What I Love about My God
13. What's a Friend For
14. God is There
15. Which Will it Be?
16. One Soul at a Time
17. Darkest Night
18. No Place for Fear
19. Heavy Heart
20. Set Me Free
21. Sure Promises
22. I Lost Count
23. Day with God
24. On and On
25. Always Safe
26. Tell Me I am Silly
27. Melt Hearts
28. Everybody Runs
29. How Many Times?
30. Blessings

31. Disappointment
32. Today's Rain
33. Safe Spot
34. Far Away Honor
35. Rare Truth
36. Content to be Content
37. Blinders
38. Shadows of Change
39. God the Artist
40. Hundred Percent
41. I've Gained
42. Lasts, Firsts, and Changes
43. Simply Everywhere
44. Dream Meaning
45. More than Silver
46. Crucify Him
47. Sands of Time
48. Rose on my Grave
49. His Mighty Hand
50. We Cried Mercy and God Delivered
51. You are Royalty
52. Plans God has for You
53. Beautiful Reflection
54. Nothing and Nobody
55. With My All
56. As the End Draws Near
57. If You Only Knew
58. Nobody Knows
59. Charge to the Class of 2009
60. Charge to the Class of 2010
61. Be Brave, Be Bold
62. He Knows Your Heart
63. Meant to Say

64. What If
65. Walk Free
66. Our Lady
67. Angel in Disguise
Story Poems
68. Heart Cry
69. The Proud Angel's Fall
70. Bound
71. The Mask
72. Sense of Death
73. Carry the Message
74. Those Days
75. Heart of a Hero
76. First Half of a Moment
77. Adern's Strength
78. My Heart Belongs in the Mountains
79. Beautiful Land
80. You Make Life All Right
81. He Leapt for Joy
82. No Body
Thank You for Reading:

1. My Champion

You are Lord in Heaven
Lord on this Earth.
Master and Maker,
King and Creator,
Father of all things,
And lover of my soul.

I have an enemy.
He knows how to hurt me.
He knows what I want to hear.
He knows how to twist my wants,
Make me think they're needs.
Help me drown out his voice.

Lord, be my victory,
Be my champion.
Show me Your glory.
Make me part of your story.
I want to know You better.
Open my ears, flood my mind.
Teach my heart to hear
You and only You.

2. On the Road of Life

Seems I've lost my way
On the road of life.
Don't know where to turn.
Couldn't turn around.
No going back now.
Biggest problem I see:
Too many paths before me.
Don't know which to choose,
Know I'll have to soon.
Cannot shake the feeling
Somehow, I've lost my way
On the road of life.
I know God's with me
I can hear Him say, "Trust me."
Funny how it's easy to swallow those words
When everything's steady
But knowing change is coming
Has me in an uproar.
Never was a big fan of change.
Still, I know God's with me.
Whenever I feel lost
I'll turn to Him
And find Him always there.

My Champion

3. Who Will You Call?

Who will you call
When dark times come?
Who will you call
When hope fades away?
Who will you call your sole strength?
Who will you rest your soul in?
No matter what darkness may lie ahead
There is only one steady source of peace.

Call on Him from your knees
So that He may say,
"Rise, my child, I am here!
Find your rest in my arms.
Life may be hard, but I'm am stronger.
Won't you please call me?
Through me, the blind will see.
Through me, the lame will walk.
Do not let a lack of vision
Blind you from my power.
I am waiting to work great wonders
In and through you.
So, won't you please call me."

4. Unfair Tale

You may not believe in fairy tales
But listen to this unfair tale.
The King over everything had just one Son.
He condemned him to pain and death
Because you and I deserved to die.

You may say, "Never me.
I'm as good a person as can be."

That may be true, but haven't you heard?
Sinners and saints alike
Fall short of perfection.
If the story ended there
It'd be quite the tragedy,
But God found a way to set us free.

Jesus's death and sacrifice
Paved the way to paradise.

Now, one and all are invited
To claim new life, hope, and peace,
To claim their place in this family,
To become true royalty.

5. Fair
(For Chrissy)

When the pain in my head
Just won't go away,
What can I say?
Hallelujah. Hallelujah. Hallelujah.

The devil would like me to believe
The pain won't ever end.
The devil would like me to believe
Nobody cares for me.

When I hear these bold-faced lies
I can only drown them out
With a chorus from my soul:
Hallelujah. Hallelujah. Hallelujah.

We were never promised fair
This side of Heaven.
Quite honestly, we can't afford fair,
For it means all stand condemned.

Our Father in Heaven determined long ago
Life wouldn't be fair.
There would be relief through Jesus Christ.
Hallelujah. Hallelujah. Hallelujah.

6. To the Captive

Though you're a captive
And you may never hear my prayer,
I will pray, night and day,
God pours peace into your soul.

Love carried you far from home to a
Place and people you do not know.
Though I've never met you
I know the more you learn
The more you love.
Don't give up hope.
For we need to hear
The life lessons learned living over there.

Your fate lies in higher hands.
I will pray, night and day,
Cooler heads prevail and one day,
This will be a happy tale.

7. Chains are Gone

Jesus sought me though I fled Him
Day and night, he whispered truth.
Though no words ever touched my ears,
My heart clearly heard Him say:
"Come, dear child, come home.
I am waiting with open arms.
Don't you know the chains are gone?
They are vanquished by my love.
Can't you taste the sweet, free grace?"

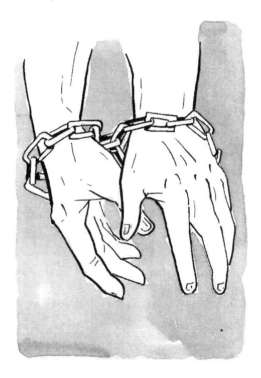

8. More Alive

When the skies are gray,
The grass looks a little greener.
When the skies are gray,
Smiles are a little warmer.
When the skies are gray,
Flowers shine a little brighter.
When the skies are gray,
Everything looks more alive!

The same holds true in my life.
When the skies are gray,
Many things that didn't impress me
Suddenly look better, brighter,
Full of hope I need.
When the skies are gray,
I cling to hope found in Christ.
This hope turns into peace
And I begin to feel more alive!

9. Place for Peace

There is a song deep inside
I must give release.
It's more like a cry:
O God, Why?
Why do these things happen?
Why can we not see the pain
That dwells in young minds?
They cry out in so many ways,
Yet we're blinded by the day to day.
They slip right through silently,
Then suddenly they're gone,
Faded like the last note of a song.

There is a place to find peace,
To find true release for all that pain.
Rest in God, weary ones.
You may think it's so easy
For me to say such things,
But I only know what I know
Because I've been where you are,
Lost and bound by fears.

10. Jesus, Father, God

Jesus, Father, God, and Holy King
Bless me, Lord, in everything.

Help me deal with all my pride.
I need you on my side.

Give me the right words to say.
I need strength for this day.

I want the world to see,
Christ Jesus shining in me.

I cannot make it on my own,
So I lay myself before your throne.

Jesus, Father, God, and Mighty King
Bless me, Lord, in everything.

11. Prayer Tonight

This is my prayer tonight:
Lord, teach me wrong from right,
Teach me what you want for me.
I will try to learn,
To read, to teach, and to discern.
Give me directions and I will go far.
Promises I break,
Mistakes that I make,
Are washed away by your blood.
Lord, haunt my every thought,
Help run this life you bought.

12. What I Love about My God

What I love about my God
Is that He loves me
More than I can see,
More than I could ever fathom.

What I love about my God.
Is that things on Earth
And things in Heaven
Obey Him.

What I love about my God.
Is that He's everywhere.
He's always there.
He never fails.

What I love about my God.
Is that He loves me
More than I can see,
More than I could ever fathom.

13. What's a Friend For

I see you look a little down today.
I hate to see you this way.
I hardly know what to say.

Cast your cares at the foot of the cross,
And as you wait on the Lord, talk to me.
What's a friend for, but to share your pain?
What's a friend for, but to keep you sane?
Now and always.

God's always there, and He always cares.
God's always there, and He never fails.
Still, He gave you friends to hold your hand.
He gave you friends to help you stand,
Through good and bad times.

14. God is There

God is there.
When everything is going right,
And life is good,
God is there.

God is there.
When your child is sick,
And you can't pay the bills,
God is there.

God is there.
When hope fades away,
And all you have is tears,
God is there.

God is there.
When you reach your goals,
And fulfill your dreams,
God is there.

15. Which Will it Be?

You must ask yourself
Which will it be?
During the easy times
It's easy to believe
That you'll always believe.
But during the hard times
Will your faith stand up?
Will you have the faith
To stand up for your faith?

16. One Soul at a Time

Lord God have mercy.
Shine down in glory.
Light up this world
One soul at a time.

Fill us with love for the lost ones.
Tune our spirits to hear
Cries for mercy.
You know what burdens
Lay heavy on hearts and minds.
Give us strength to break every chain.
Hopelessness. Helplessness.
Fear, pain, and loss too deep for words.
Take it away. Far, far away.
Replace it tenfold with hope
and peace too deep for words.

Lord God have mercy.
Shine down in glory.
Light up this world
One soul at a time.

No darkness can stand
Where your words are heard.
So fill our voices with your praise.
We'll tear down the walls
Surrounding the lost ones
And call them to come home.
Fill us with boldness.
Fill us with brightness.
Use us to light up this world
One soul at a time.

17. Darkest Night

May the peace of God rest deep in you,
So you will walk on through this pain.
What words can cover for such a loss?
We've heard it all before.
Pain fades with time.
Heavy loss means lots of love.

Though I have been there before
And walked on through,
I remember asking God.
In the dark of night,
In the coldest parts of life,
Will I hear your voice whisper to my soul,
"Everything will be all right."?

With the advantage of hindsight
I see He was always there.
In my darkest night
In the coldest parts of life.
He lent strength and hope to my soul.

My Champion

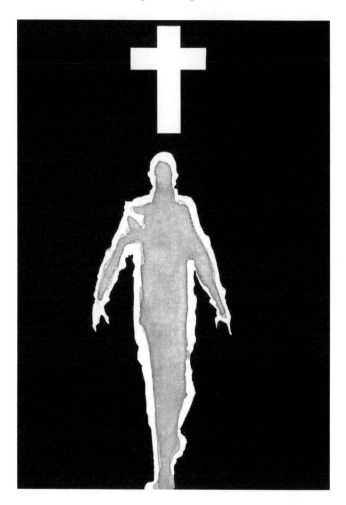

18. No Place for Fear

Life flies on by.
There's no stopping it.
Sometimes it's easy.
Enjoy those times,
For they may not last.
Do not fear,
For the Lord is near.
And when the Lord is near,
There's no place for fear.

19. Heavy Heart

Sometimes, I find my heart heavy
For I don't know how to reach you.
If you don't reach out to me,
I don't know what you need from me.

I can take no steps
If I don't know where to find you.
It's like shouting into dark
And hearing nothing,
Only to find out sometime later,
You were there the whole time,
Bound and gagged by helplessness,
Close enough to touch by hand,
But far away in mind and spirit,
And far beyond my reach.

Tell me, how can I reach you?
Is there some middle ground
We can safely tread?
Can we cross the distance
That lies between us?

Sometimes, I find my heart heavy
For I don't know how to reach you.
If you don't reach out to me,
I don't know what you need from me.

20. Set Me Free

Sweet Jesus, set me free.
Satan just won't let me be.
I'm a prisoner to my sin,
And I don't know where to begin.
I know I need you in my life.
Please help me through pain and strife.
Come into my heart today.
Let there be no further delay.

Sweet Jesus, you set me free,
Though Satan didn't want to let me be.
Thank you for everything.
It makes my soul want to sing.
You took my sins on you,
Washed me clean, and made me new.
.

21. Sure Promises

I know not what troubles you,
But keep the Lord in your sight
And everything will be all right.

Put your hope in the Lord.
Then come what may,
come what might,
He will help you through darkest night.
Each hard day will fade away.

Worry not to fail or fall
For He makes sure promises:
"Lean on me throughout your life.
I will walk beside you
And carry you when needed."

I don't know what tomorrow brings,
But I have learned to trust God.
He never ever fails or falls
All through trials I hear His calls,
"Trust me, my child."

22. I Lost Count
(For my mother)

On this Mother's Day,
I would like to say:
Thank you for everything you do.
Long ago, you took a child
And raised her to love the Lord.
I don't think there's a better
Gift you could give.
I know you didn't do this alone,
But this isn't his special day,
This is Mother's Day.

I lost count of the ways
God used you to touch me.
I lost count of the things
You taught me.
I lost count of the times
You picked me up, dried my tears,
And held me close after a fall.

I would try to count the ways,
But I wouldn't finish
For a thousand days.
All that's left to say is
Mom, I love you.

My Champion

23. Day with God

Today, I spent the day with God.
I watched the clouds come down
And touch the mountains.
I saw the sun dance on tiny waves.
I think I needed this day.

Whether it was the hour of prayer,
The sunlit walk, the quiet time,
Or the chance to clear my mind …
I think I needed this day.

I spent the day with God.
No matter where my life will lead
I want to spend more days with Him.

24. On and On

I wanted a commander.
Someone to guide me.
Someone to tell me
Where to go, what to do,
Who to help, and how to act.
Instead, I got God.

How can I describe Him?
He's so much greater than I could imagine,
He is loving, kind, majestic,
Magnificent, glorious, perfect,
Holy, honorable, and beautiful,
Mighty, awesome, and gracious.
I could go on and on.

If I used every word mankind made,
I would barely begin to describe Him.

God has many roles to fulfill.
He is Master, Creator, Life-giver, Savior,
Hero, Father, Friend, and Teacher,
Counselor and Comforter,
Peacemaker, Judge and Healer.
Once again, I've only begun.
I could go on and on.

25. Always Safe

You know I have an active imagination
Because you gave it to me.
It is a source of endless joy,
As it takes me far away.
But at times, it is a source of worry
Because I can clearly picture
Everything going wrong.
Through it all, I will remember:
I am safe in Your arms.
I am safe until You let me go.
Since that day will never come,
I will always be safe.

Though I make many mistakes,
You never stop loving me.
You know every time I fall away
Yet You draw me close anyway.
Through hard times
I will always remember:
I am safe in Your arms.
I am safe until You stop loving me.
Since that day will never come,
I will always be safe.

26. Tell Me I Am Silly

Tell me I am silly.
Tell me I worry too much.
Tell me my fears are only dreams.
See, I fear not for me,
But I worry for those I love.
My imagination likes to run wild.
It is a blessing and a curse.

Every unaccounted moment
Brings up fears that they'll die
And leave me all alone.
I know that's silly.
So, tell me I am silly.
Tell me I worry too much.
Tell me my fears are only dreams.

God, I beg You
Never let these fears come to pass.
Come be my peace of mind.
Tell me I am silly
Then post Your presence
As guard of my heart.

27. Melt Hearts

Do not fear
What the future holds.
Nothing can hold you captive
If you believe.

I believe:
Prayer can set wrongs to right,
Melt hearts made of stone,
And heal brokenness.

I believe:
Love, hope, and peace
Are treasures to cherish
When darkness, hardship, and heartache
Try to sink your spirits low.

28. Everybody Runs

Everybody runs. Everybody hides.
Everybody tries to say
It's not their fault.
But the truth remains:
Our sins are hard to miss.
Only God's love can save us.

Why do people run?
Why do people hide?
Why do people try to say
It's not their fault?
When the truth remains:
God's love is hard to miss.

O Lord, thank you for being
Patient with my wayward heart.
You whispered, "I love you."
Until I finally accepted
It as truth.

29. How Many Times?

I do not know
How many times
In this life
I will fail.

But I do know
That every time
I can return to the foot of the cross
And receive my redemption.

I will bring the broken pieces
Of my spirit to the Lord
And He will make me whole.

30. Blessings

I have food, friends, and family
Yet these pale in comparison
With the greatest gift:
God's Son.

I cling to hope for a bright future.
I must remember
Where the blessings come from.

Thank you, Father, for loving me,
Even before I drew a breath.
Thank you for the many blessings
That have made my life so grand!

31. Disappointment

Sometimes life sends me flying.
I'd be lying if I said this
Doesn't disappoint, but I understand
God's got something better in mind for me.
At this time, I just can't see
That future unfurled.

I'd be lying if I said this doesn't disappoint.
I wish I could see my future.
I wish decision-making was much easier.
Heck, while I'm at it,
I wish I never had another worry.
But that's not the way life works.
I am glad that I know God
For of the two of us
He's the one who knows what's going on.

When life sends me flying,
I can fly free and clear in mind,
Knowing He's ready to catch me,
Set me on my feet, and lead me by the hand.

32. Today's Rain

Nothing's really wrong today,
But rain's got my spirits down.
Rain makes the flowers grow,
But that doesn't make me like it.
It possesses a dark, dreary power
That bids me go to sleep.
At the same time, I find the soft
Splatter of rain versus ground, soothing.
Rain makes the grains grow
And that sort of makes me like it.
Thank God for the rain.

God made the rain.
Now, that makes me like it.
Rain pulls my spirits down,
But God pulls my spirits up.
Feeling down makes it easier
To sense God's presence.
The blessings outweigh the emotional low.
I'll thank God for the rain
Because it waters my soul today.

33. Safe Spot

I know I put it in a safe spot.
The only problem is that I
Do not remember where that is.
I know it's in a safe spot.
So safe, even I can't find it.
This is driving me crazy.
I've got to stop doing this
If I want to keep my nerves intact.

Too safe's gonna make me
Find it too late.
I know it's not the end of the world,
But it sure is irksome.
The thing I want to find
Is a little too safe for me.

34. Far Away Honor

All I want to do is worship the Lord
With prayers and deeds
And writings that please Him.

I want to let my mind
Conjure up worlds far away,
Where people encounter problems much
Like ours and discharge
Their duties honorably.

We've let honor and duty
Fall to the wayside,
But in worlds far away,
I can bring both back,
In flashes of light, and justice by might.

One day, honor will return to Earth,
For the end game's written:
God wins.
Choose whom to serve.

35. Rare Truth

God loves us.
This is one rare truth.
Christ died for us.
This is another rare truth.
Both are basic Christian knowledge.
I wish to speak on a third rare truth.

Quickly, we forget God is Holy.
We forget that He's always listening.
Often, we let our tongues rule us.
One minute, we're praising God,
And the next, we're cursing, like fools.
Our hearts are so fickle!

I wish I could say it was different for me,
But my heart also wanders.
I don't lack fervor,
But who and what I call master varies.
One minute, I'm serving God,
And the next, I'm serving self.

I wish I could grow out of this,
But I fear it shall always be
A wearying battle for me.

36. Content to be Content

There are a great many dreams
I wish to see come true.
But for now, I am content to be content.

That doesn't mean I won't
Fight for my dreams with
Prayers and deeds and writings on hope.

Though I am content to be content,
I'm more convinced than ever
I have a calling to fulfill.
Idle musings about where this will lead
And what the cost will be
Will never deter me for long.

When I feel weary, I will pray.
I will arm myself with knowledge.
I will practice to no end.
I will push myself to the edge
And cast myself over, knowing full well
I'll land in His arms and there I will be
Content to be content.

37. Blinders

Why are we not better off
Than in ages past?
Terrorists scare us. Vows mean nothing.
Murders are confined to page fifteen.
People do whatever they please.
In a time when morals
Get defined by individuals
There's a shortage of good.
Part of me wishes for the past
When people knew they were bad.
They were defiant in their sin,
But at least, they didn't rationalize.
Deluded people are hardest to reach.
"That's good for you but not for me,"
Is ten times more infuriating than
"Just leave me to my sin."
Lord, save us from self-imposed blinders.

38. Shadows of Change

I could tell you many a sad tale
Concerning the shadows of our past.
Tales of woe, darkness, pain,
Where our heroine's nearly slain.
Her beaten body draws our eyes,
Her broken spirit tugs our hearts,
Her overthrown mind, saddest of all,
Awakens pity pure and deep.
Why's this tale sound so real?
Could it be we've heard this before?
What good is sympathy if
Our minds can't fathom change?

Some were born to privilege
Yet remain blind to it.
You and I may agree to disagree
On a great many things,
But let us not waste time debating.
Those given much have much to give.
Sometimes, the best gift is an open heart.
What good is sympathy
If our minds can't fathom change?
Hear these tales, picture change,
Move your heart first, then the world.

39. God the Artist

Did you know God's an artist?
This world shows God's an artist.
Have you seen a baby,
Soft and sweet, full of life,
Made unique by God's hands?
Have you seen the ocean?
Heard the waves pound the surf,
Wondered where they come from?
Have you watched the sunset
From the heights of a mountain?
If you had then you'd know
God must be an artist.
Have you heard the birds
Sweetly summon the sun to shine?
Have you seen the forests
Clothed in cheerful colors?
I could go on forever.
So many sights and sounds declare
God must be an artist.

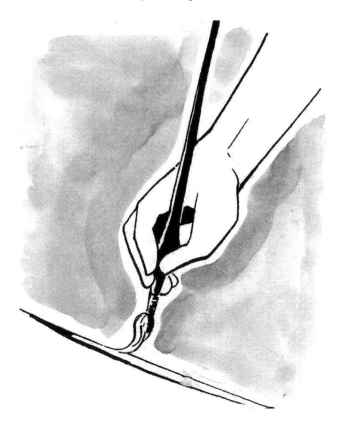

40. Hundred Percent

Idols come in many forms.
If something consumes your mind
And isn't God, it could be sin.
See, it ain't easy being pure.
See, it ain't easy measuring up.
There's a hundred percent failure rate.
Where's the hope in that?

There's always hope.
There's a hundred percent certainty
Jesus Christ died to set us free
From sin's sinister shackles.
Won't you claim this freedom?
Live your life striving to be good.
Fight evil within and without
With all you are.
Don't be surprised when you fall.
If you surrender this fallen you
God is ready to work on your heart.

41. I've Gained

I had somebody ask for my help today.
It was a most unusual request.
I forget her exact words,
But the essence of the message was:
"Pray for my friend,
You do not know her,
But worse, she doesn't know our Lord.
This is a tough time of transition
Would you pray for my friend?
Would you reach out to her?
She doesn't know our Lord."

Well, what could I say?
"Of course, I will pray.
I hope God will help me find your friend.
I see she is on your heart."

What kind of friendship
Forms such compassion?
I think I want that.
I think I've gained something
Better than gold today.
I've gained a friend I may never meet.
I've gained new reason to send up prayers.
I've gained so much, now it's time to give.

42. Lasts, Firsts, and Changes
(college graduation)

Now that I know the next step
The burden of waiting is finally gone.
It's a year for lasts, firsts, and changes.
I do not do well with these.
Still, I hope in hard times
Of waiting, not knowing, or changing
My faith will shine brighter
And stronger than all my impatience.
It's a time for lasts, firsts, and changes
What a wonderful time to live.

There is something extra cheerful
In the sunshine this time of year.
How I wish these days
Could go on forever!
Since I cannot stop the lasts,
Firsts, and changes,
I will trust in and praise God
For He has all things well in hand.

43. Simply Everywhere

There's a world between you and me.
I may not know what assails your mind
And though I've never felt the pain you do,
I'll cross this distance
On the wings of my prayers
And I'll hold you in my mind
Like one holds a crying child.
In Christ, the distance fades away
For the One we serve is
Neither here nor there, simply everywhere.

There's a world between you and me.
Though it seems the struggle may never end
Thought you'd like to know
How much you inspire.
Not by your strength but simply faith.
I see my Master in the works of your mind
And I want to join that work.
So, I'll cross this distance
On the wings of my prayers
And together we'll praise the One
Who is neither here nor there,
Simply everywhere.

44. Dream Meaning

Am I dreaming?
If I'm dreaming, leave me sleeping,
I find I like this pretty dream.
I saw something I only ever saw
In my mind come to life today.

If I'm dreaming leave me sleeping,
I find I like this pretty dream.
As I touch this dream,
Hold it in my hands,
I'll praise the Lord Most High
For He gave me this dream.

Now that it's come true
I'll pray His blessings
Rain down on me,
For only in the Lord
Was this dream ever
Meant to mean anything.

45. More than Silver

I see you wear a cross,
A tiny piece of silver,
Hanging from a chain.
Do you wear it as a charm,
Or does it mean more?
Jesus Christ, God made flesh,
The only one to fully conquer death
Made the cross so much more than silver.
His love manifested in grace
Leads lost souls to life.

The cross can be
A tiny piece of silver
Hanging from a chain
Or it can mean so much more.
Life in Christ may be
As painful as living without
But His life gives us hope
That though the towers of today
May still be fragile,
The cross is so much more than silver.

46. Crucify Him

Deep in a dream
I heard myself scream,
"Crucify Him!"

I woke with a start,
Stricken in heart,
Surprised to find my eyes
Wet with tears.

I silently begged sleep to return,
Knowing it was not meant to be.
I needed to think.
The dream haunted me deeply.

Finally, I realized that every time
He gave me directions,
I defiantly cry, "Make me!"

I might as well be crying,
"Crucify Him!"

With this realization fresh in my mind,
I made my peace with God,
Falling into a deep, sweet sleep
Before my smile faded.

47. Sands of Time

Come watch the sands of time
Sweep on by.
Though sense says
Hold on to all those dear
We face this journey without fear.

Come watch the sands of time
Sweep on by.
All good sense inquires:
Why cling to fruitless pride
When time may not be on your side?

Come watch the sands of time
Sweep on by.
Truth be told boldly.
There may be substance to fears.
Tears may pave the way through years.

Come watch the sands of time
Sweep on by.
Let not sorrows rule
For hope will always remain.
Though things will never be the same.

My Champion

48. Rose on My Grave

I have seen too many people
Pass from this life
To think I'll escape unscathed.
Life can change in a moment
Or end in a flash.
While we're on this topic
I have some questions for you.
Will you place a rose on my grave?
Will you be among those I count a friend?
Just one rose placed on my grave
Will mean somebody knows.
For not much in this life I fear
But one thought can haunt me
I fear of fading into dark
Alone.

49. His Mighty Hand
(For Areck)

The work of His mighty hand
Shines through you
Your servant's heart has served
Many people very well.
You may never know
What heart's you have touched
With a simple smile or well-placed word.

His mighty hand rests upon you
May it guard you from disappointment.
May it carry you through all manner of pain
To the day you will gain
Crowns to cast at His feet
When we will sing glory to the One King
Whose mighty hand rests upon you.

He has done great things with your soul.
We will watch and wait with great hope
For life's play to move forward.
We will watch and wait to see
Where His mighty hand will take you
And what great things He can do
Through one willing servant's heart.

50. We Cried Mercy and God Delivered
(For Bernadette)

As our hearts crumble
With deep-seated sorrows,
We take hope in a promise.
God knows all our tomorrows.

We cried mercy and God delivered.
It was not the way
We would have wished it.
So, now we cry for mercy:
Great God, deliver us from this pain.

Though we weep
For the one who fell asleep,
Someone wise once told me
One day we will see her
And even hear her say:
"What took you so long
To come home?"

Long before we thought to cry mercy,
God healed the world through his only Son
So that we who cry mercy
May know true peace through Him.
We can take hope in this promise:
Every time we cry mercy
God will deliver.

51. You are Royalty
(For Kaiwen)

I've known you less than a thousand days,
Seen you less than half of that.
It's been a privilege to know you this long.
Though I could do without some hardships
I would not change one day of my life.
Hopefully, you can say the same.
My hope and prayer for you is this:
Let God work His will in you.
Day in and day out if you listen
You will hear Him speak quiet words.

No one knows the hour or day
Our Lord will come to claim His own,
Go forth and seize upon
Every chance to shine His words
In thought and deed.

Indeed, if you let Him wholly reign in you,
No trial, no hardship, nothing at all
Can hold you back.
There will be nothing your spirit lacks.
When something tries to bring you low
Remember who you are.
You're a child of God,
You are royalty.

52. Plans God has for You
(For Taylor)

You may not know exactly
What plans God has for you,
But you know inside it's true:
God's got a plan that will unfold
Like a story untold
When the time is right.
Hold Him in your sight.

When you leave this place
Please hold a space
In your heart and mind
For those left behind.

We do not know exactly
What plans God has for you,
But we know inside it's true:
You're in good hands.
No matter where you land
No matter what you face
No matter how you run this race.

Cling to truths learned here.
Face the future without fear,
Knowing none of life's demands
Can ever steal you from God's hands.

53. Beautiful Reflection
(For Cristina)

When I think of you
The word *beauty* comes to mind,
In and out I find
You're a beautiful reflection of God.

Cool, calm, and quiet sometimes,
More often bursting with passion,
May your love of life always serve Christ.
Continue to be a beautiful reflection of God.

Many a day passed by
I regret I did not try
To know you better.
You're a beautiful reflection of God.

Never lose that fire inside
Nor attempt to hide
The gifts God has lavished upon you.
You're a beautiful reflection of God.

There will be days
Set against you in many ways.
When doubts try to take you low
Remember who you are
And who you reflect inside.

Nothing at all can forever claim
Someone sealed in His name.

54. Nothing and Nobody

Heard there was young
Woman ready to end her life
Though it's barely begun.
Seems it's a story told
Too many times these days,
So many times, it kind of gets old.

As I get older
My heart gets colder
I must remember to pray:
"Lord, melt this ice away."

I've been thinking kind of hard.
Think I'm ready to provide
Conclusions:
When it comes right down to the core
Everybody needs nothing and nobody
But the Lord God Almighty
On their side.

55. With My All

When I look at you
Fear for the future
Fades, for then I remember
Everything from that first September
To the present and far beyond
Has passed just as God planned.

You are beautiful, intelligent, unafraid
Of giving your time and talent, unpaid.
The works of your mind and heart
Will be sorely missed as you depart.
I could go on and on
About the many ways you're a paragon.
It's been a pleasure to watch you grow
I wonder where God will have you go.

Please remember to always pray:
"Dear God, lead me day by day
Take my mind and mold it.
Fill me with Your Spirit!
Give me ears to hear Your call
To pray and praise You with my all."

56. As the End Draws Near
(For Victor)

Not so long in the past
You asked me for a song.
At the time, I could not
Grant your request.

As the end of your time here draws near,
I feel drawn to say farewell
In a way you'll remember well.

We've heard the songs
That draw you nearer to God.
May that gift born deep inside you
Never fail to praise His name.

As the end draws near,
It's my hope and prayer
That each of us learns how to praise
God with heart, mind, and soul.

May it be that every day
Our hearts rise to say:
*Here I am, Lord, take my spirit
Make me more like You today.*

57. If You Only Knew
(For Mark)

Did you know?
Nearly every word said
Could be turned into a song
If you only knew how to
Make it work for you.

Any thought, any phrase,
Any feeling locked inside
Can be given new form.
If you only knew how to
Make it work for you.

To some extent such a thing
Can't be learned in a class.
You must learn it from life.
Everything, good or ill,
Holds a lesson inside
If you only knew how to
Make it work for you.

Every day take some time to pray:
"Dear Lord God, help me find
Every word, every phrase,
Every feeling You want unlocked.
Take this gift placed in me
Use it for Your glory.
May my only goal
Be to bring You praise."

58. Nobody Knows
(For Alyssa)

One could hardly call you shy.
I can't remember a day gone by
When a smile has failed to grace
Your lovely face.
Did you know your strong
Spirit could pull people along,
Out of the depths of despair
By letting them know you care?

Nobody knows what tomorrow may
Bring your way:
Trials or triumphs or unknown pains.
Seems sometimes we keep sane
By pushing all thoughts away
And simply living day by day.
I know you know you need not fear
But I feel I should be clear:
God knows your heart, mind, and soul
And what you need to keep whole.

Praise God in good times
When things works out fine.
Other days, cling to this truth:
Life may not always be smooth
But God is God through it all.
Listen closely, you'll hear His call:
"Reach those headed for a hungry grave
It was for them I died to save."

59. Charge to Class of 2009

You may leave and never look back,
But I hope you will not lack
For fond memories of all you've done,
Though your life has barely begun.
Every end births something new.
There's not much else to do,
But reflect upon the things you know.
Prepare to enter the world and sow
Seeds of truth and seeds of light,
Set the world's wrongs to right.
Moment by moment, day by day
Find the will inside to pray.
Lord, your grace knows no end.
Give me wisdom to defend
This fragile faith.
I need strength to cling to what is dear
To your heart and to your mind.
Help me help others find
This peace surpassing all knowledge
For such is my privilege
As a child of the One King.
There are countless other reasons to sing
Your praises all day long.
May every act for good become a song
Of praise to You.

60. Charge to Class of 2010

It will long be my fervent prayer
That you take life with a care.
Guard your eyes and ears
Lest the things that slip by lead to tears.
I know it is easy
To think *never me,*
But the world's whispers and shouts
Are enough to sow many doubts.
So many innocent minds walk out that door
Unguarded and wind up spiritually poor.

It will long be my fervent prayer
That you take life with a care.
Never thought I'd be back.
Found my life on a far-away track,
Not necessarily right or wrong,
Just that I found I didn't belong
In that place, in that time.
In the end it worked out fine
Because God had a plan for my life,
One great enough to carry me through strife.

It will long be my fervent prayer
That you take life with a care.
Trust the Lord in everything
So at the end of time you can hear Him say,
"Well done, my good and faithful servant."

61. Be Brave, Be Bold
(For the Class of 2011)

You will go far in this life.
Whether your role is to change
A thousand lives, ten times that, or only one,
May the Lord's hand of mercy
Reach through your life and shower love
On those who surround you.

You won't be perfect, not by far.
We were not asked to be Christ,
Only to let Christ be Christ in us.

As you leave this place,
Be brave, be bold.
Hold tightly to the truth.
It may not seem epic
From where we're standing,
But we are locked in a battle
For the souls of mankind.
So be brave, be bold,
Hold onto this truth:
In the end God wins.

62. He Knows Your Heart

When you're weary, without rest,
When you're ready to fall apart
In a moment's time,
Sing praise to the Holy One,
Sing praise to the only one
Who knows your heart
Better than you do.

He knows what fears haunt your dreams.
He knows each tear you shed in secret.
No motive you have ever held
Deep within your mind
Can change the simple facts:
He died to rise to love you more.
He died to rise to save your soul.
He died to rise to give you rest.

When you're weary, rest in Him.
When you're ready to fall apart
Sing praise to the Holy One,
Sing praise to the only one
Who knows your heart
Better than you do.

My Champion

63. Meant to Say
(For my grandmother, Miriam Smith)

Captured in a child's mind
There exists a pretty picture.
I remember many stairs, a fancy church,
Afternoons spent outside climbing tires.
Ten summer visits blending into one.

Do you remember the shy smile I wore
When my heights triumphed over yours?
I think you shrank more than I grew,
But I'm allowed some delusions.
I digress…
I really meant to say,
"I wish I had ten thousand words
To express how I love you
But why waste words when three will do?
I wish I had ten thousand years
To expound on how I love you.
You are a precious person
I'm blessed to know."

64. What If

Sometimes you come upon
A place to choose a new path.
A glance down the past road
Leaves you wondering what if …
If only you could have known
Where every road would lead.

A peek down the current choices
Leaves you wondering what if …
the future whispered its secrets.
Make sure these "what ifs"
Don't leave you paralyzed,
Afraid to move on,
Unable to go back and start again.

If you could borrow courage
Enough to take one step
You would find the future easier to claim.
You would find some peace
And solace in this knowledge:
No matter where you have been,
What you have done,
Who or what has hurt you along the way,
The next step belongs to you.

65. Walk Free

Father, Prince of Peace,
Lend me strength to release,
This need to control my fate.
Help me to wait well.
I sometimes wonder why
You who placed the stars so high
Would descend to this place
To save a fallen race.
A child, a king, a ransom.
That's a steep price to pay.

If we listen, we can hear your call:
"Come sinners, one and all.
Come near, dear child.
Come claim your inheritance
Leave nothing to chance.
Darkness, pain, and fear
Have no more place here.
Your debt is paid in full.
Walk free.
Taste true life as it should be."

66. Our Lady

Have you come to see our lady?
She stands next to the sea.
How many have come to see our lady?
Countless strangers are inspired by her.
She hails from distant shores
Standing for timeless values.
She holds words of freedom in one hand
A bright torch to light the way.
Have you come to see our lady?
For a hundred years or more
She has graced our shore
Offering hope to desperate thousands
Wandering here to begin new lives.
As you gaze at her strong face
Let your worries wash away.
Though heartache may follow,
Hold onto hope.
When you're weary think of our lady.
Have you come to see our lady?

67. Angel in Disguise
(For my friend, Jenny)

Anyone ever tell you you're an angel?
Maybe not a real one but real enough
To the thousands who see
Christ's love in you.
You can hide it with humility
But it shines ever brighter with every prayer.
Your small acts of kindness go a long way.
Though others may not see your deeds,
They are tiny little seeds
Sewn into the hearts of the needy.
Your well-timed smiles and gentle spirit
Have carried wounded souls
To the only source of lasting peace.
There's hardly a greater victory.
That makes you a hero.
That makes you an angel in disguise.
Of course, not a real one
But real enough to the lives you touch.

68. Heart Cry

There was a time in my life
When all was simply strife.
You don't know how far I've come
To find safety and true love.

How was I to know
You were here all the time
Waiting and watching,
Hungry for my heart and soul?

It may sound trite,
But now I clearly see
I was not completely me
Until I knew you.

I feel I could face anything
Now that I know you
Will watch and wait,
Keep me safe from true dark.

Before this very moment,
I felt quite the lonely captive,
But here with you holding me
I at last feel truly free.

69. The Proud Angel's Fall

He was the most beautiful of all the angels.
And he had power to be sure.
Then, one day, he said, "I should be God."
And a third of the angels agreed.
He was cast from Heaven.
Now, he is lord over Hell.

There's a lesson to be learned here.
No matter how beautiful you are,
No matter how powerful you are,
Always remember who created beauty,
And who gave you power.

Take pride in working for the Lord,
But always remember God is God,
Only He has the right to reign
Over everything.

70. Bound

Among the many mistakes that I have made
The most painful is falling in love with you.
Thought I could change you.
Thought I could claim you for the truth.
I see I lied to me.

I know you love me
But my heart is not free.
I'm bound by belief to serve the Lord.
If only I'd listened to His teachings.
Maybe I'd save us all this heartache.

I know you love me
But your heart is not free.
You're bound to the world.
The closer you draw
To the gods of this world.
The farther you'll be from me.

Don't you see we serve different masters?
I disobeyed mine; look where it got me.
I'll make it right now.
It's the most painful thing to me
But I know I must flee,
Before my heart is bound to you again.

71. The Mask
(A poem based on Nadia Ayers)

I am a prisoner to my thoughts.
Who can free me?
I am trapped in a tower.
There is no entrance,
No exit, no escape.
Fear and frustration build up.

I wear a smile as a mask.
Can you read the pain I feel?
My family means everything.
My siblings and I have many Gifts.
We can and will change the world.
Not much world-changing
Happens peacefully.
Some will hunt us.
Some will fear us.
Some will hate us for no reason.

I wear a smile as a mask.
Can you read the pain I feel?
I can read strangers' thoughts
But I cannot control hearts or minds.
Love will have to rule.
My siblings know me best.
The future's uncertain,
But my loyalty will always
Belong to family.

72. Sense of Death

How could the king
Abandon us by his death?
Where are the honors due the fallen queen?
This place reeks of death.
I need no other clues or accounts.
A sense of death surrounds you,
Poisoning the air.

Few truly know the truth.
Fewer still are brave enough
To speak out against this injustice.
A sense of death surrounds you,
Poisoning the air.

It's no wonder they keep their silence
They must have more regard
For their life than I have mine.
I cannot keep silent.
Kill me if you will.
A sense of death surrounds you,
Poisoning the air.

I will add my voice to the whispers
Speaking against the wrongs done here.
A sense of death surrounds you,
Poisoning the air.
Can you feel it closing in?

73. Carry the Message

I went to the Captain and announced,
"I'm tired of being on the sidelines!
I want to be of use in these hard times.
Captain, please give me another task,
For I am tired of watching others.
They gain glory and honor,
While I tend their horses!"

The Captain nodded and said,
"That is the task I have set for you,
But if you wish more, consider this,
Every task is worthy of honor,
And glory comes from how you perform.
Go! Carry the message to the troops."

I merely nodded, sad and confused.
I went for a walk deep in thought.
"How is a stable boy as good as a soldier?
It is not fair that we are at war …"

Then, I walked past the wounded tent.
One man lay on his cot and prayed,
"Bless the Captain for this task,
Allow me to fulfill my duty well."

I waited for the soldier to finish.
Curious, I asked,
"Sir, what is your task?"

He smiled and said,
"I am to encourage the soldiers,

And write them letters, lad."

"Is there honor in that?" I wondered.

The soldier looked at me kindly.
"Lad, we have peace and rest,
But many are not so lucky.
We have good news to share.
Others must know that we still care.
To sharing this is a glorious task.
There are many to hear,
But few to carry the letters."

That day, I received my commission.
Now, I too carry the letters
To those hard at work.
There are even missives
For those who have not heard.
My new task is to tell of the King
And encourage the soldiers.
"The enemy had fled in many places."

74. Those Days

I remember the days
When we walked the halls of heaven,
Hand in hand, heart in heart,
Our minds as one.
Do you remember those days?
Days of exploring the land.
Days of creating from dawn 'til dusk.
Everything new, everything good.
Tell me you remember those days.

Tell me you remember …
The day we discovered the meaning of life.
The day we shared love for the first time.
The day we made the sun stand still
Just because we could.
Carefree days, careless days.
What would I give to return to those days?
The could have beens,
The should have beens,
They haunt me.
I think a season or two slipped by
While I did nothing but cry
For what we had, what we lost,
And everything in between.
Do you remember those days?

75. Heart of a Hero

Tears fall and purge my eyes.
My heart aches such that I must speak.
Woe to the maid in love with a hero.
There lies a hero near unto death,
And here I flee as he bid.
Curse my promise to live.
Part of me prays Spirit let him live
One more day, one more night,
Part of me wonders, would it matter?
For such is the heart of a hero
To throw himself in death's way.
It was my life he saved this day.
I know for sure, had he lived
He'd be right back in this war
For he had the heart of a hero.
Even in death he'll live on
For love bids me take his fight.
The heart of hero must never die,
And it never will so long as love is a word.
For such is the core of hero's heart.

76. First Half of a Moment

Sunny days and starlight,
Smiles and faces of friends held dear,
Are locked within my mind,
Bright and clear.
I am terrified that one day
They will fade away.

The last things I saw:
A red light, a black car,
Flying glass, and my own hands
Will be forever blazed into my mind.

People complain their lives are so busy.
They just want to slow down,
Take a breath, and start over.
Be careful what you wish for,
For everything can change
In the first half of a moment.

The last things I saw:
A red light, a black car,
Flying glass, and my own hands
Will be forever blazed into my mind.

I wanted a change of pace,
But this is crazy.
How could I have known that
In the first half of a moment,
In the space between heartbeats,
My vision would be forever
Confined to what I remember?

Julie C. Gilbert

All is darkness and cold loneliness,
Wish I could see the faces around me.
Please don't cry.
It hurts enough as is.
All is strange and new,
So daily, I'll replay the scenes:
Sunny days and starlight,
Smiles, and faces of friends held dear.

77. Adern's Strength
(Published in *Reshner's Royal Ranger*)

Nehkermah stenmielsto
Keqwirco seikero.
Sehnomfreh.
Sehstimorea.
Nehnqwirm seikero.
Sehnawbon.
Sehnomorikan.
Nehnqwirm seikero.

No fiery danger striking near my heart
Can kill or conquer, when I have love.
See how it floods me.
See how my strength grows.
Nothing can conquer me, when I have love.
See how it binds every wound.
See how my strength rises from ashes.
Nothing can conquer me, when I have love.

78. My Heart Belongs in the Mountains
(Based on *Reshner's Royal Ranger*)

See where the mountains reach up
And kiss the sky,
That's where you'll find me.
My heart belongs in the mountains.
Though I wasn't born there,
So many years went by that I
Couldn't imagine life anywhere but there,
Yet the more I'm around you
The easier it is to forget
My heart belongs in the mountains.
Every time I close my eyes
I can clearly picture you,
Your ice blue eyes, warm smile, rich laugh—
I must forget or go crazy!
How many times must I remind me?
My heart belongs in the mountains!
I know you know I love you,
And I've felt the same from you.
Is it enough to cross the distance?
Maybe one day you'll come find me.
Just go where the mountains reach up
And kiss the sky
That's where you'll find me.

My Champion

79. Beautiful Land
(Based on *Reshner's Royal Guard*)

Beautiful land,
You hold much power over me.
See, you have my heart and soul
Just as you have my body
Locked here by gravity.
My dreams go no higher than your peaks,
No farther than your seas.
Once or twice they brushed the stars,
But always my thoughts returned home.

Wish I could spend my days and nights
Wandering hills, fields, and forests.
Duty may keep me palace-bound,
But one day I'll climb a mountain
Or walk by the sea for hours,
Listening to it whisper
Or rage as the case may be.
Until that day, dreams will do.

Beautiful land,
Do I love you because you're home,
Or are you home because I found
Love here?

80. You Make Life All Right
(Inspired by *Reshner's Royal Guard*)

Sleep well, little princess.
Dawn will come soon.
Don't you know? You bring hope to my life!

May the night hold peaceful dreams.
May the morning's light shining on you
Bring a smile to your eyes.
When those blue gems light from within
Worry fades away.
Sleep well, little princess.
Don't you know? You make life all right!

Storms may be coming.
The thought of wind leveling
Land from shore to shore
Almost sinks my spirits low.
Then, I remember you
And worry fades away.
Sleep well, little princess.
Don't you know? You make life all right!

War may be coming.
The thought of chaos reigning here
Almost drowns my soul with despair.
Then, I remember you and worry fades away.
Sleep well, little princess.
Don't you know? You make life all right!

81. He Leapt for Joy

When Elizabeth heard Mary's voice
The baby within leapt for joy.
He leapt for joy
Because he knew
The one who walked his way
Would one day bear a son,
And that boy would be
The Savior of the world.

He leapt for joy
Because he could do no less
In the presence of the King.

Filled with the Spirit
Elizabeth cried out,
"Blessed are you among women
Blessed be the child you will bear!
But why am I so favored,
That the mother of my Lord
Should come to me?
As soon as the sound of your greeting
Reached my ears
The baby within leapt for joy."

He leapt for joy
Because he could do no less
In the presence of the King.

82. No Body

As was foretold long ago,
Our Lord was cruelly crucified,
And so, the grave would be satisfied.
After the deed was done,
They laid his body down,
Deep down in a garden tomb.

Three days later,
As the sun rose on a new week,
Women took spices to the tomb,
But they found no body.
Just some strangers dressed in clothes
that gleamed like lightning.

They found no body.
Just some strangers with a crazy claim:
"He has risen."

You can believe me
Or walk away,
But you can't change
What happened that day.
They found no body.

Thank You for Reading:

I hope you enjoyed reading this Christian Inspirational poetry collection. While reviews are awesome, let's do something different. If something in here touched you in anyway, share it with somebody else.

What does that mean? God has given everybody gifts. If you paint, paint. If you sing, sing. If you draw, draw. If you bake, bake, and so forth. Put the phrase or title or even a whole poem (if applicable) on your labor of love and use it to bless somebody.

It does not have to be shared on social media, and in some cases, it shouldn't. However, if you do, use #MTPchallenge if you choose to share via social media and tag me if you like. I'm on Facebook, Twitter, Instagram, and Mewe.

If you'd like to try some fiction, check out my website (**juliecgilbert.com**). Many stories can be experienced in ebook, paperback, or audiobook.

Hop on the newsletter if you want to keep up with life and new release news.
(https://www.subscribepage.com/n7e8l8)

Sincerely,
Julie C. Gilbert

Printed in Great Britain
by Amazon